BLACK CUILLIN RIDGE SCRAMBLERS' GUIDE

Sgurr nan Gillean and the gorge from the approach to Coir'a'Bhasteir.

Black Cuillin Ridge Scramblers' Guide

S. P. BULL

SCOTTISH MOUNTAINEERING TRUST

BLACK CUILLIN RIDGE SCRAMBLERS' GUIDE

First published in Britain 1980 by
The Scottish Mountaineering Trust   Edinburgh

Copyright © 1980 S.P. Bull

SBN 906227 10 0

Designed, produced and sold by
West Col Productions
Goring   Reading   Berks.   RG8 9AA

Printed in England by Swindon Press Ltd
Swindon   Wilts.

Contents

Illustrations

Uncredited photos are by the author

Maps and diagrams, see route listing at end of book

Cover photograph by Donald Bennet

ACKNOWLEDGMENT

The author wishes to express gratitude to all the friends
who joined in the exploration of the Cuillin which lead
to the production of this guide. In particular thanks are
due to Heather Monie who shared all the scrambles and
climbs; drew the diagrams; wrote the Flora; and without
whose assistance and encouragement the guide would
never have been written.

Introduction

CUILLIN is the term for a hill range in the south-west part of the Island of Skye. Both the spelling and the meaning of the word are the subject of debate but "Cuillin" seems to be the most accepted spelling and many authorities believe it comes from the old Norse for a keel-shaped ridge (Kjolen). Its more general use is to describe the main ridge of the Black Cuillin which stretches for about 13 km. (8 miles) from Sgurr nan Gillean near Sligachan in the north to Gars-bheinn in the south. It has some 20 tops over 914m. (3000 ft.) and the ridge never descends below 762m. (2500 ft.). It is mainly composed of a dark rock, gabbro, which is particularly rough, making it a paradise for the rock climber. Indeed, it is without doubt the best place in Britain for ridge-wandering and one of the best for climbing. Unlike the mainland peaks which have their hard routes but also easy ways up for the walker, there are peaks in the Cuillin accessible to the rock climber only, and few can be ascended without use of the hands.

There is another smaller group of hills of similar type, east of the main ridge and sited between the south end of Glen Sligachan and Loch Slapin. The highest top of these is Blaven (Bla-bheinn, 927m., 3042 ft.).

The other hills of the area are often called the Red Cuillin because of their colour. They are quite different, for while they too are bare and rocky, they are rounded mountains composed mainly of granite and covered in scree. They suffer in popularity from their impressive neighbours but elsewhere would be highly regarded as they provide fine walking. The western group lies east of Glen Sligachan with Glamaig 775m. (2537 ft.) their highest top. The eastern group are on the far side of Blaven between Loch Slapin and Broadford.

This guide is concerned with the more restricted group of the main ridge, the Black Cuillin. It is almost entirely a narrow, shattered rock crest of peaks, pinnacles, dips and clefts. It lies in a great C formation, most of it encircling Loch Coruisk on the east, though the ridge of Druim nan Ramh comes down to split off the top part, Harta Corrie. On the outside of the C there are a number of side ridges or spurs which form the great corries along the west side.

There are a total of 21 named summits in the main ridge, listed below with an indication of their accessibility by the easiest route.

Main Ridge Summits

*Sgurr nan Gillean	965m.	3167 ft.	Hard scramble
*Am Basteir	936	3069	Moderate scramble
Basteir Tooth	916	3005	Rock climb
Sgurr a' Fionn Choire	935	3068	Walk
*Bruach na Frithe	958	3143	Walk
Sgurr na Bhairnich	861	2826	Easy scramble
An Caisteal	830	2724	Moderate scramble
Bidein Druim nan Ramh	869	2850	Rock climb
*Sgurr a' Mhadaidh	918	3012	Easy scramble
*Sgurr a' Ghreadaidh	973	3192	Moderate scramble
Sgurr Thormaid	927	3040	Easy scramble
*Sgurr na Banachdich	965	3166	Walk
Sgurr Dearg (cairn)	978	3209	Easy scramble
* Inaccessible Pinnacle	986	3234	Rock climb
An Stac	953	3125	Easy scramble
*Sgurr Mhic Coinnich	948	3111	Hard scramble
Sgurr Thearlaich	978	3208	Hard scramble
*Sgurr Alasdair	993	3257	Easy scramble
Sgurr Sgumain	947	3108	Easy scramble
Sgurr Dubh na Da Bheinn	938	3078	Easy scramble
*Sgurr Dubh Mor	944	3096	Hard scramble

8

Caisteal a' Gharbh Choire	829m.	2719 ft.	Rock climb
*Sgurr nan Eag	924	3031	Easy scramble
Sgurr a' Choire Bhig	875	2872	Walk
Gars-bheinn	895	2935	Walk

An asterisk* indicates a Munro, one of the Scottish peaks over 3000 ft. originally listed by Sir Hugh Munro in 1891. There are about 280 of them in the whole of Scotland and some climbers have ascended them all.

In the list above, Sgurr Alasdair, Sgurr Sgumain and Sgurr Dubh Mor are not actually on the main ridge but they are very close to it. Two of them are Munros and Sgurr Alasdair is the highest peak in the Cuillin.

WINTER CONDITIONS

The hills of Skye lie close to a sea warmed by the Gulf Stream and so they rarely become gripped by snow and ice like many of the mainland peaks. On the occasions when severe winter conditions transform the hills like their mainland counterparts, most of the expeditions described in this guide become serious undertakings calling for full winter mountaineering skill. Even when free of snow, the Cuillin in winter are less enjoyable for the scrambler than many other areas, partly because of the short winter days, but also because of the particular ferocity of the wind. The force of the wind in these mountains, sometimes even in summer, is a major hazard; in winter, right up to Easter, it can make them unapproachable for days on end.

WHERE TO STAY

There are two main centres. Sligachan, with a hotel; camping is possible but there are no facilities. Glen Brittle, with a climbers' hut, youth hostel and a campsite. Camping is not allowed elsewhere in the glen.

Carbost is a possible base but this involves driving to reach the start of all excursions and the drive down to Glen Brittle is time consuming. Climbers prefer to stay at Glen Brittle because of its easy access to the great climbing area of Sron na Ciche; drinkers tend to stay at Sligachan.

ACCESS

Unlike many of the Scottish hills there is little or no grouse shooting or deer stalking on the Cuillin; therefore problems of access do not arise. Sheep are grazed on the hills and dogs should always be kept under control, especially in the lambing season; sheep often lamb a long way up on the hill. There has been a lot of nuisance from dogs and a number of sheep have been killed or injured.

NOTES ON USE OF THE GUIDE

Most visitors to the Cuillin arrive by road at the north, or Sligachan, end and may then drive or walk round the west side of the ridge to the south or Glen Brittle end. The ridge is therefore described from north to south, approaching in every case from the west side. Even when dealing with Coruisk, access is described from a base on the other side for it is assumed that those who stay at the Coruisk Hut, or who camp nearby, are already familiar with the Cuillin.

Each peak, corrie, spur and bealach (pass) has been described, first with a general note, then at greater length for those interested. The practice throughout has been to give more detail for the easy routes as these may be selected by those with least confidence.

Standards

In the descriptions each scramble has been graded. This may be irritating for the experienced because all the routes are graded "easy" by rock climbing standards. However, many of the routes are not literally easy, sometimes even by climbing standards, and drawing distinctions within the very wide "easy" classification should assist those in need of guidance in this matter.

When the term "walk" is used it means that for those with reasonable balance and experience the route can be done with hands in pockets. In reality nothing described in the guide is a walk in the normal sense of the word. In the Cuillin it involves boulders, scree, heather and considerable effort; suitable boots and clothing are essential.

"Easy scrambling" entails using hands for balance and assistance. "Hard scrambling" implies some shortage of hand- or footholds and the route here may demand the sort of moves which, if it were sustained at the standard, would make it an easy rock climb. Availability of useful holds more frequently depends on reach and manoeuvrability than the tall and young realise. One of those assessing the standards used in this guide is only 5 ft. tall so that the grading is seen through the eyes (or perhaps at the end of the arms) of the short and not so young; others MAY find some of the scrambles easier but they should not be found more difficult. For an idea of comparability, Striding Edge (Helvellyn) is mainly a walk with one short section of moderate scrambling. Crib Goch (Snowdon) and the Aonach Eagach (Glencoe) contain some hard scrambling moves, though much of the ground is walking or easy scrambling.

Time

One of the problems for the mountaineer in Skye is the difficulty in estimating how long an expedition will take. Weather conditions, composition of the party and the fitness of individuals cause this to vary but experienced hillmen can make a rough estimate adjusting for these factors. It is worth remembering that whether you calculate by Naismith's rule or have your own formula the Cuillin do not fit it. The times given here are based on averages taken by the author's parties over many years. A lot depends on physique, age and ability, but the times quoted are consistent. Those with little experience should allow longer until they are sure of their speed. Route times allow for the odd photograph and boot relacing but do not include extended stops.

On the rare days of set fair weather the dry, warm gabbro is unbelievably adhesive and time seems to stand still. How different it is when the holds are wet and greasy; you are stiff with cold and the wind destroys all balance. Strong men have been seen on hands and knees on an excursion graded a "walk" when conditions were bad enough. The rainfall in Skye is considerable. There is real truth in the comment of Sheriff Nicolson:

> If you are a delicate man,
>> And of wetting your skin are shy,
> I'd have you know, before you go,
>> You had better not think of Skye.

Some mountaineering guide books assume the weather to be good, or that you have gone fishing. If you do that in Skye, especially in the usual holiday months, you do a lot of fishing. Unless suitably experienced it is obviously foolhardy to venture on the hills in adverse conditions, but routes which might be possible on a bad day are identified in the guide. Remember that if you miss the way and cannot see clearly ahead, in the Cuillin the alternatives tend to be impossible cliffs and huge drops. At best, to find a way down may mean the long, long trek back from Coruisk.

Grading applies to dry rock. A thorough wetting slows your pace, makes route finding difficult and sometimes dangerous; it makes the rock slippery and saps your energy. Even the splendid gabbro is not unaffected; its pitted surface affords holds for vegetation so that it may become greasy like any other rock in damp conditions. The basalt and dolerite, which make up half the range, including Sgurr Alasdair itself, are positively fiendish.

Compass bearings

Two major factors cause many people to get lost on the Cuillin and, in particular, to end up at Coruisk. One is that it is possible to go scrambling along an apparently clearly defined ridge ahead, only to discover later that in descent it was not so clearly defined after all. The area round Sgurr Dubh na Da Bheinn is notable for this. In more rounded hills loss of bearing is sensed earlier.

Secondly, the compass is badly affected by the magnetic property of the rock. Even when you could rely on it you feel you dare not trust it. Bad deflections (up to 180°) occur all along the main ridge with the exception of: summit of Banachdich, Bealach Coir' an Lochain, Bealach Coire Lagan and Bealach na Glaic Mhor. Nevertheless, parties are recommended to carry a compass. You cannot work to fine bearings but these are not always necessary in the Cuillin where it is usually a matter of a general direction to pick up a ridge. Take readings from several points; try to keep below the highest place and away from large rock masses, including cairns. With the compass unreliable, build up your own notes of what it does and does not do for you.

An altimeter is a useful instrument in Skye. It, too, is not altogether reliable because the pressure changes; but if constantly checked against known heights it can make a contribution. Finally, carry a notebook. There is a tendency to change terrain and direction frequently and a note of key points seen on a fine day may become invaluable on a bad one.

Directions

The terms "left" and "right" are given to refer to your left or right as you proceed on your intended route. In ascent, left means left as you go up; in descent, left means your left as you go down. A stream is always in descent and so the convention is to describe a stream's right bank as the "true right". The same location in your ascent would be referred to as the left bank as it would be on the walker's left hand.

Heights

These are taken from the latest (1965) 1:10,560 Ordnance Survey map and are given in both metres and feet in this present transitional phase. The tourist 1:25,000 map has 25 ft. contour intervals labelled in metres. A table at the back of the guide will enable the reader to convert a contour marked in metres to its equivalent in feet.

MAPS AND BOOKS

O.S. maps

1:25,000 Outdoor Leisure map "The Cuillin and Torridon Hills" covers the whole area. Grid sheet no. NG 42/52 is more convenient in size but it omits the southern end for which another sheet is required. Because of the rugged terrain these maps are not easy to read above the 600m. contour and a magnifying glass will be found valuable.

1:50,000 grid sheet no. 32 is not adequate for mountain work but this covers the entire area for general purposes.

All O.S. maps are in a transitional stage in converting to metric measurement. At present these maps have the contours in feet but labelled in metres.

S.M.T. map

1:15,000 Black Cuillin of Skye. 1977. Useful and attractive map for studying the area and route planning but it has no contours. The old three-inch map was withdrawn in 1978.

S.M.T. Guidebooks

"The Island of Skye" by Malcolm Slesser. District guide series, 1975. Under revision. This is essential reading for an appreciation of the island as a whole and it covers such matters as weather, geology, birds and mammals, as well as details of some of the rock climbs.

"Cuillin of Skye" by J.W. Simpson. 2 vols. Rock climbing

series, 1969. Under revision and being replaced by the "Skye and the Small Isles" new series climbing guide.

General Books

Amongst the many topographical books written about Skye, the most interesting for the hill walker and scrambler are long out of print. These include "The Cuillin of Skye" by B. H. Humble (Hale, 1952) and "The Magic of Skye" by W. A. Poucher (Chapman & Hall, 1949). The latter includes some useful photographic notes as well as fine pictures but it is something of a collector's piece today.

Geology: There is a very clear introduction by G. S. Johnstone in the S. M. T. guide. A useful book on the whole of Scotland for those whose interest is just beginning is "Geology and Scenery in Scotland" by J. B. Whittow (Penguin, 1977). Those with some geological knowledge will be able to make use of the British Regional Geology handbook, "Scotland: The Tertiary Volcanic Districts" by J. E. Richey (H. M. S. O, 1961).

Flora: A check list of the plants of the islands of Skye and Raasay is entitled "A Botanist in Skye" compiled by C. W. Murray and obtainable from the Botanical Society of Edinburgh, and Skye Tourist Information Office.

SUGGESTED EXPEDITIONS

Those who are intent not only on the ridge may also have time to enjoy some of the walks which give splendid views of the mountains. The boat trip from Elgol to walk round Loch Coruisk is recommended. The walk up Glen Sligachan takes you right into a wild and rugged area. The track over the Bealach a' Mhaim is a fine vantage point for the north end of the ridge. From Glen Brittle visit the point of Rubh' an Dunain. Forestry Commission tracks often make good walks; especially suggested is the way up from Glen Brittle over the Bealach Brittle to Loch Eynort.

For strong walkers who are prepared to toil up scree or

rough ground, the ascent of many of the corries is very rewarding - Tairneilear, Mhadaidh, Ghreadaidh, Lagan and possibly Ghrunnda. The ridge can be gained by the scree path up Fionn Choire, after which you might continue to Bruach na Frithe. Another way to attain a summit is by the toilsome scree of Coir' an Eich to reach Sgurr na Banachdich. Very long, very rough but still only a walk, is the ascent of Garsbheinn, and you might go along part of the main ridge from there.

Many walkers will be prepared to go on to try some of the easier scrambling and so the following are suggested: Bruach na Frithe by the north-west ridge; Sgurr nan Gobhar to Sgurr na Banachdich; Sgurr nan Eag.

It is often a good plan to begin with exploration of the corries. All the main corries are available to the scrambler but Coir' a' Bhasteir and Coir' a' Ghrunnda are recommended. The following expeditions all contain easy scrambling: Bruach na Frithe and down Sgurr a' Bhasteir; Sgurr na Banachdich from Sgurr nan Gobhar and down Coir' an Eich; Sgurr Sgumain from the shoulder of Sron na Ciche and down Coir' a' Ghrunnda; Sgurr Alasdair by the Stone Shoot; Sgurr Dubh na Da Bheinn; Sgurr Dearg; the summit of Sgurr a' Mhadaidh from An Dorus.

Those wishing for harder scrambling will find various possibilities in the round of Coir' a' Ghreadaidh; Sgurr nan Gillean by the Tourist Route; also Sgurr Dubh Mor.

o

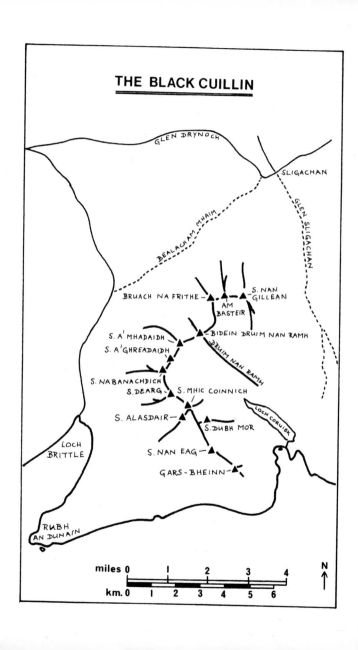

THE BLACK CUILLIN

Main ridge traverse

This expedition is strictly for rock climbers. It normally involves setting out from a bivouac at one end and traversing the whole ridge in one go. The ridge is only about 13 km. (8 miles) long but there is some 3000m. (10,000 ft.) of ascent. Most parties commence from Gars-bheinn in the south and go towards Sgurr nan Gillean in the north as the climbing is more natural in this direction. Fit and experienced parties reckon on a very long day, that is about 12 hours on the ridge itself.

Once considered impossible, the ridge traverse was first completed by Leslie Shadbolt and A. C. MacLaren in 1906 in a time of 12 hours 20 minutes from summit to summit. Since then times have become shorter and numbers have increased. The story of it, and of the Greater Traverse which includes Blaven and Clach Glas, makes fascinating reading. There is a very high failure rate amongst those who undertake the expedition. Something of a pointer to likely achievement can be gained by assessing knowledge of the ridge; how well it has been explored; where caches of supplies and water might be placed, and so on. Climbers have been known to set off and just do it; the great J. M. Edwards was one. Doing it thus on sight is rare and for people of a certain calibre. Ordinary mortals get to know the ridge, go over the harder bits and prepare thoroughly.

Starting from the south all is easy until the climber reaches Caisteal a' Gharbh Choire. Slings rotting at the north end indicate those who failed to notice that the climb down from this knobble descends on the west side and not over the north where there is an overhang. Then there is easy going but route finding problems over Sgurr Dubh na Da Bheinn; in mist many find their way to Coruisk from here. After Bealach Coir' an Lochain a pinnacle is reached which forms one side of the Thearlaich-Dubh gap. It is usual to abseil down the harder short, or south, side of the gap and climb up the very polished north side which is now graded V. Diff. and is about 25m. (80 ft.) in length.

Arriving on Thearlaich it is customary to nip across the scree to take in Sgurr Alasdair, as it is the highest top, even though it is not on the main ridge. Now back over Thearlaich and down its crest to the end where descent to the bealach is slightly on the Coruisk side. Then comes the ascent of Mhic Coinnich which is best done by the open corner called King's Chimney (Diff.). 70 ft. If the airy traverse of Collie's Ledge is taken it is necessary to go back over a sharp crest to reach the summit. To omit it is not really "doing the ridge". Likewise the climber must go up and over the disgustingly loose An Stac and then the Inaccessible Pinnacle.

By now there may be problems of sore feet, tiredness and shortage of water, for there is none anywhere along the ridge. There are no further climbing problems all the way to Sgurr a' Mhadaidh.

The summit of Mhadaidh is a 10m. (30 ft.) slab, tilted on its edge to make a narrow crest. From the north end the route needs care as the WNW descent to Thuilm has to be avoided. The route trends right, or eastwards, past or preferably over a pinnacle, then rises to the second top (usually called 3rd as they tend to be numbered from the north end). This includes a short slab taken on the west side (Mod.). Most of the next top requires climbing (Mod.) in ascent where it is taken direct. After that it is rough scrambling over the NE Peak and down to the Bealach na Glaic Mhor.

Then comes an exasperating peak for those who have not been there before. Bidein Druim nan Ramh has three tops which form a triangle and cause changes in direction in its traverse. It is very confusing in mist. From the south there is a scramble over the West Peak, then it is best to climb directly up from the dip to the Central Peak. Loose ledges on the south-east side are an alternative. There is a very airy slab leading away from the summit and downwards, first on the east side, then on the west until arrival at the overhang. Here it is a pleasant climb down over a slab, then a short wall (Mod. Diff.) on the Harta Corrie side; some abseil it. Reference to avoidance by a traverse on the west appears problematical by the amount of rock sent down by parties on it. Arriving at the dip, the North Peak is ascended by a dyke going left, then upwards. Attempting to go straight up, or holding the dyke for too long, causes difficulties. The climber then comes easily down the slabs of the north ridge.

After Bidein he is away again, scrambling all the way to the Basteir Tooth. This is one of the major problems. As part of the ridge it must not be avoided. It is usually climbed by Collie's "Ordinary Route" which descends towards Lota Corrie to come up the south-west edge in slabs and chimneys for 125m. (400 ft.) to the top (once Mod., now Diff.). Alternatively it can be ascended directly from the bealach by Naismith's South-West Face Climb (Diff.), across the face and up to the top dramatically. The route is not obvious and the details should be studied in the S.M.T. guide. There are still two further pitches, including an awkward overhang, to reach the top of Am Basteir. Having overcome this problem, a scramble leads over the summit and down to the bealach.

Finally one has to go round the Gendarme and go up the West Ridge of Sgurr nan Gillean and descend, usually by the Tourist Route, though some continue to Sgurr na h'-Uamha (Hoo-a) as a final flourish.

If you are not a rock climber, or you do not think you could do all this in one go, take heart! Those who have completed the whole traverse feel a tremendous sense of achievement, but most of them talk in terms of endurance and perseverance and they agree that to enjoy the ridge, to savour it, to appreciate it fully, you need to take your time over it. The experienced scrambler can do just that. Most of the ridge can be covered in five or six expeditions and in these this unparalleled chain of mountains can be thoroughly enjoyed. Six expeditions would be:

Sgurr Alasdair

Sgurr nan Gillean by the Tourist Route

The round of Coir' a' Ghreadaidh

Sgurr Dearg to Sgurr Mhic Coinnich

Gars-bheinn to Sgurr Dubh na Da Bheinn with the addition of Sgurr Dubh Mor.

Am Basteir, back to the bealach, round under the cliff and along the ridge to An Caisteal.

This would only omit: the full traverse of Sgurr nan Gillean; the ridge of Sgurr a' Mhadaidh; the Thearlaich-Dubh gap. You would have by-passed An Stac and the Inaccessible Pinnacle; the peaks of Bidein Druim nan Ramh; the Basteir Tooth. All the same you would have acquired a very close knowledge of the ridge and it would be something to savour again and again, that is the disease called "Skye Fever" for which there is no known cure. In the sub-species "Cuillin Fever" it is very virulent.

o

Geology

A knowledge of the geology of the Cuillin is fascinating even for those who have not studied it in detail. Stand on the ridge and guess which way the glacier went to carve these magnificent crests and hollow these great ice-worn basins, a mere 10,000 to a million years ago. Equally exciting is to realise that this gem of all the mountain areas of Britain, with its quietness and serenity, was formed by a vast period of volcanic turbulence before that.

The main formation of the rocks of Skye happened in geologically recent times. Volcanic activity poured huge thicknesses of molten rock over an area far larger than the island but which can be seen in the basalt moorland of the north.

Later there was further activity, centred on volcanoes within the locality, though no peak which you can see today bears any direct connection with these. This produced a lava, chemically similar to the basalt, but one which cooled slowly beneath the surface. It is, therefore, much coarser-grained, which together with its uneven weathering, produces the rough and adhesive qualities of the gabbro. One variety of this is the even more adhesive peridotite which mainly occurs in An Garbh Choire, the bealach and the top of Coir' a' Ghrunnda, across Sgurr Dubh na Da Bheinn, and into Coir' an Lochain: there are outcrops elsewhere. This ginger-brown rock, which is so destructive to the hands, is even more coarsely crystalline and weathers to a sponge-like appearance.

Thirdly, a quite different molten rock, an acid granite, was heaved up. This has a pinkish colour and weathers more evenly so that, when worn into shape, it forms the more rounded Red Cuillin.

More molten rock, basalt and dolerite, intruded the gabbro in vertical dykes and horizontal sheets called sills. The dyke rock is hard and brittle, and tends to fracture and therefore erodes more quickly than the surrounding gabbro. This causes the formation of gullies and chimneys, such as Waterpipe Gully, and to make the channels in which some of the burns run their straight course. Occasionally it is the dyke which remains; the example often cited is the Inaccessible Pinnacle, though this is partly gabbro sandwiched between two dykes and perched on a dolerite base.

The sills originate from a centre north-east of Coruisk. If you think of an inverted cone centred there, you will be able to imagine the lie of these sheets which average 45° but get steeper toward the centre and less so further out. They give the Cuillin that peculiar list toward the middle of the C shape of the range and give rise to the slabs inclined towards Coruisk which are such a feature of places like the north end of An Caisteal, the North peak of Bidein, and the "wart" on Sgurr a' Ghreadaidh.

It is the uneven rate of erosion where the sheets meet the surface which produces much of the serrated appearance of the ridge. In the north, the dip toward the centre has cut the ridge of Sgurr nan Gillean to form the Pinnacle Ridge. Along Sgurr a' Mhadaidh, which runs almost east-west, the tops tend to be steep on the west and more gently inclined on the east. On Blaven and Clach Glas the dip is down towards the west, but it is north on Sgurr na Stri. The sheets, which are mainly of dolerite, vary both in thickness and in hardness so that in some places they erode and in others they stand out from the gabbro. This means that sometimes the crest of the ridge is formed by the sill. As the dykes often form the chimneys by which a cliff is climbed, so the line of the sill may form a useful weakness, as in Collie's Ledge.

Unfortunately the fine-grained basalt and dolerite are much

more unreliable, splintery rocks and are slippery in the wet. It is well-known that most of the Alasdair-Sgumain area is basalt, and at the south end of the ridge the summits of Sgurr a' Choire Bhig and Gars-bheinn have basalt caps.

The present form of the range is the result of the erosion which took place after these rocks were laid down. Most of the sculpture occurred during the ice-age when glaciers covered the area. It was ice which gouged out the corries and over-deepened some to hold lochans, like Lagan, Ghrunnda and Coruisk. Glaciers moving over the rock smoothed it into the rounded, but scratched, slabs seen so well in these same corries, and which dumped odd blocks of rock in strange places. As they moved inexorably down they tore away the rock to leave the sharp ridges which are such a delight to the scrambler, and the steep headwalls as the playground for the climber. Then came the frosts to shatter these ridges into crests and pinnacles and to mantle it all with scree.

The work of the frost goes on, even today, so that after the winter a new rock fall is often observed. Since the ice-age, water has been the main shaper of the scenery. Snow and rain carry scree, earth and vegetation downwards. The burns slowly splash away even rock, as can be seen in the Allt Coir' a' Mhadaidh, and having worn a path for themselves, they may take a new direction, as in the approach to An Dorus.

Talk is of the eternal hills. The change is slow but this landscape is one where these changes can be traced and contemporary ones recorded. The effect of the changes make the Cuillin what they are.

Bird life

For those who are not birdwatchers, the following notes are the author's observations about the most likely sightings you may have about the Cuillin during the main holiday period.

Everyone who goes to the highlands hopes to see a Golden Eagle but many of the claims to have done so arise from anything from a corvine to a Buzzard. It is always safer not to claim a sighting unless really sure; nevertheless, there seem to be relatively more eagles on Skye than on the mainland. If you get a good view, the really helpful sign is the size. A two metre wing span contrasted with a sheep should leave you in no doubt. Otherwise look out for the dark colour and the light head of the mature adult, though the juveniles have white on the wings and tail. They tend to be silent birds. An eagle has a large territory so they can turn up anywhere.

You may be lucky enough to see other birds of prey but only the Kestrel and the Buzzard are very likely. The latter's plumage is variable but their mewing cry is quite distinctive. Ravens with their characteristic "pruk, pruk" are almost certain, and so are the oddly marked Hooded Crows with their black wings and heads and almost lilac coloured bodies, though these are officially termed "grey".

Red Grouse are reported to be sparse in the area but they do nest on the moors. Higher up, Ptarmigan are there too, but not in large numbers. In their summer plumage of grey-brown anoraks and white climbing breeches they are an unmistakable sight.

On the moors, too, you may well hear the plaintive pipe of the Golden Plover as they stand on a hummock of peat distracting you from their young, but their brown plumage and black bellies make them difficult to see with the naked eye. In the lower, wetter areas you have a good chance of hearing the "chip, chip" of the Greenshank, or to flush the long-billed Snipe into its zig-zag flight.

All over the area, except the tops, little brown birds "pheet, pheet" around you, starting out of the grass at your feet. These most characteristic of British mountain-country birds are Meadow Pipits. They look like small Larks, which you will also see. Likewise the white rump of the Wheatear: a handsome bird with grey back, buff underparts, black eyestripe and the "white arse" from which it gets its name.

On the lochans look out for the Red-Throated Diver which breeds there and feeds on the sea. Frequently its quacking can be heard as it flies over, and also its mournful wail as it calls to its fellows. Try not to disturb it in the breeding season as numbers are reported to be small. On the burns there are Dipper, Grey Wagtail (yellow underneath, not the ubiquitous Pied Wagtail), and nearby there is frequently the handsome Stonechat, betrayed by his call like two stones being struck together.

At ground level all sorts can turn up and washing lines at the Glen Brittle campsite have had regular visits from Twite, Stonechat, Whinchat and Meadow Pipits. Beyond, in the long grass, the invisible Corncrake rasps on like the winding of an alarm clock.

On all the shores, especially Loch Brittle, a variety of waders will be found; Oystercatcher, Curlew, Ringed Plover, Turnstone and Dunlin being the most likely in summer. Round the corner the Common Sandpiper will probably be found amongst the rocks.

Finally, on "off" days when you can take a walk out to the Point, Rubh' an Dunain, a birdwatcher's feast can be expected. Shag and Eider are certain. The spectacular plummet of the fishing Gannet, a never-to-be-forgotten experience, and quite frequent, too. Tern, Kittiwake, Black Guillemot are all very probable. Take your binoculars for over 7500 Manx Shearwater nest on Rum and they are frequently seen literally shearing the water, especially in late summer as the young prepare to leave the home waters.

In fact, take your binoculars with you in the hills. Not only will they help identify birds, watch deer and other wildlife, but also they prove very useful in spotting cairns, routes ahead and even watching other climbers on the crags and crests.

Sgurr nan Gillean and Am Basteir from Sligachan.

Flora

It is often said that the Black Cuillin is not distinguished for its mountain plants. This is not surprising for much of the rock is the hard gabbro which breaks down into blocky, hostile scree. However, unless very familiar with some of the renowned mainland areas, you will find plenty to see, especially where there is dyke rock or peridotite; some species in considerable profusion, some are true rarities. The Alpine Rockcress (Arabis alpina), for example, has its single British location high in one corrie.

Do not be tempted to gather specimens for almost all our mountain plants are "at risk" from the erosion of many feet, if less so today from collectors. An apparent wealth in a small area can give a very false impression.

In the north and west of Scotland many montane plants, more usually associated with habitats above 610m. (2000 ft.), colonise lower ground, even approaching near to sea level. The moorlands and coastal cliffs of Skye, bordering the Cuillin, are no exception and many such plants may be found on a lowland walk. Exploring the headlands you have a chance to see: Mountain Everlasting (Antennaria dioica), Alpine Lady's Mantle (Alchemilla alpina), little cushions of Moss Campion (Silene acaulis), and where there is a bluff of rock, Roseroot (Sedum rosea) and Dwarf Juniper (Juniperus communis nana). Growing close by are more typical moorland and bog plants: the beautiful and vanilla scented Lesser Butterfly Orchid (Plantanthera bifolia), the rare to Skye Bog Pimpernel (Anagallis tenella), all three species of Sundew (Drosera rotundifolia, angelica and intermedia) and the Pale Butterwort (Pinguicula lusitannica) of the west coast. For those with greater knowledge there is a wealth of sedges, rushes and ferns to be found in the many and diverse habitats.

Up in the corries, too, there are a variety of flowers to brighten a long ascent. Some have rather specialised needs: Mountain Sorrel (Oxyria digyna) whose colourful foliage shows up against the scree; Globe Flower (Trollius europaens) in damp and shady corners; Least Cudweed (Gnaphalium supinum) in the few places where snow lies late into the year; at least one highly successful but half hidden colony of the rare Alpine Saxifrage (Saxifraga nivalis), and Purple Saxifrage (Saxifraga oppositifolia) whose large pink flowers may festoon an isolated cliff as soon as winter is past.

Where open ground has patches of friable soil, the pioneers of the Cuillin flora are to be found: Northern Rock-cress (Cardaminopsis petraea), Stone Bramble (Rubus saxatilis) and Alpine Saussurea (Saussurea alpina) whose beautiful blooms brighten many a ledge in late summer. All these grow and flower here in a quantity unusual in the Scottish Highlands.

Three particularly rewarding areas which should give you a fair idea of the range and extent of the flora are: Coir' a' Bhasteir and Fionn Choire; Coir' a' Ghrunnda and both sides of the Bealach a' Gharbh Choire; the area between Loch Brittle and Soay Sound.

o

Conservation

A guide like this is written with misgiving for it may help people to explore areas so far little penetrated and could devastate this remote and relatively untrodden ridge into the same sorry state as many of the more well-known peaks elsewhere in Britain. The appeal to all who enjoy the Cuillin is that they leave behind them a ridge unspoilt by their pleasure on it. Litter means your litter, however wet, or tired, or triumphant you may be. When numbers are large - and numbers in the Cuillin have already reached these proportions - it not only means paper, bottles and cans but also that which can spoil a situation for those following. This includes items like orange peel, half-eaten sandwiches and, more particularly, the pollution left by those who cannot be bothered to kick a hole in the peat or remove a boulder. Some even foul the foot of climbs or a sheltered bivouac needed by someone in difficulties.

Wildlife also needs your concern. There are many species of bird, including the majestic eagle, who seek out these wild and lonely places. Having seen them, look, then go away quickly, especially in the breeding season; if they are harassed they will depart and not return. Likewise with the flowers; Skye is not noted for its flora but it does include some rarities. Many species are no longer to be seen because of the rapacity of earlier generations. Many are at risk today because of the sheer weight of numbers of those who have pleasure in the hills.

For whatever reason these hills are enjoyed, there is a sense of gratitude that they are there. The Cuillin are not just a rock gymnasia for climbing and scrambling, they are a unique ecological community of flora and fauna and rock formations.

They have a peace and a beauty all their own which enthralls all who come to know it. Those who are glad that it has not been denied to them must see that it is not denied to those who follow.

Coire na Creiche with the ridge from Bruach na Frithe to Sgurr a'Mhadaidh. The lower peak in the centre is Sgurr an Fheadain, cleft by the Waterpipe Gully.

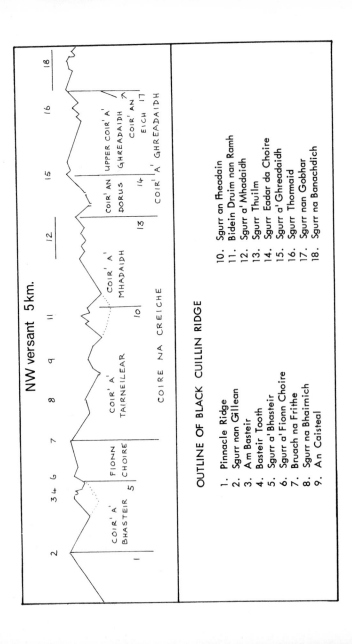

NW versant 5 km.

COIR' A' BHASTEIR

FIONN CHOIRE

COIR' A' TAIRNEILEAR

COIRE NA CREICHE

COIR' A' MHADAIDH

COIR' AN DORUS

UPPER COIR' A' GHREADAIDH

COIR' AN EICH

COIR' A' GHREADAIDH

OUTLINE OF BLACK CUILLIN RIDGE

1. Pinnacle Ridge
2. Sgurr nan Gillean
3. Am Basteir
4. Basteir Tooth
5. Sgurr a' Bhasteir
6. Sgurr a' Fionn Choire
7. Bruach na Frithe
8. Sgurr na Bhairnich
9. An Caisteal

10. Sgurr an Fheadain
11. Bidein Druim nan Ramh
12. Sgurr a' Mhadaidh
13. Sgurr Thuilm
14. Sgurr Eadar da Choire
15. Sgurr a' Ghreadaidh
16. Sgurr Thormaid
17. Sgurr nan Gobhar
18. Sgurr na Banachdich

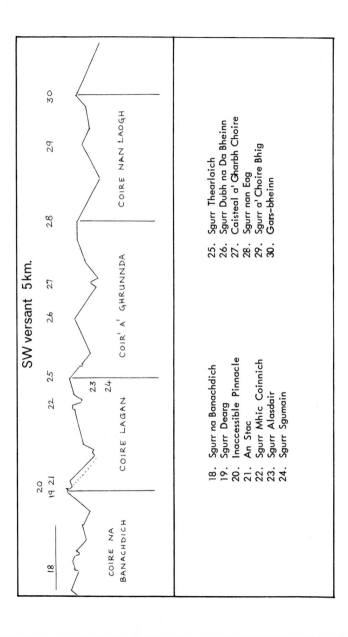

SW versant 5km.

18. Sgurr na Banachdich
19. Sgurr Dearg
20. Inaccessible Pinnacle
21. An Stac
22. Sgurr Mhic Coinnich
23. Sgurr Alasdair
24. Sgurr Sgumain

25. Sgurr Thearlaich
26. Sgurr Dubh na Da Bheinn
27. Caisteal a' Gharbh Choire
28. Sgurr nan Eag
29. Sgurr a' Choire Bhig
30. Gars-bheinn

COIRE NA BANACHDICH

COIRE LAGAN

COIR' A' GHRUNNDA

COIRE NAN LAOGH

Routes

1 Sgurr nan Gillean   965m.   (3167 ft.).

(Scoor nan Gheel-yan) Peak of the Young Men.

This shapely peak at the north end of the Cuillin greets you at Sligachan as you go along the road from Broadford to Portree or Carbost. It lies 4 km. ($2\frac{1}{2}$ miles) across the moor from the hotel; elegant and pointed as a mountain should be. To the right, or west, lies the triangular shape of Sgurr a' Bhasteir, its nearness overemphasising its importance, while between them but further away, rise the curious shapes of Am Basteir and the Tooth.

The left-hand skyline is the south-east ridge and includes the so-called Tourist Route by which the reader of this guide will probably reach the summit. On the right is the west ridge, though its famous Gendarme cannot be seen clearly from here. Stretching straight down to Sligachan is the Pinnacle Ridge with its four rock towers but they are difficult to distinguish from this angle unless mist silhouettes them.

To reach the summit the scrambler must use the Tourist Route, first climbed by Professor Forbes in 1836 and for many years the only way visitors to the island ascended the mountain. This does not mean it is a walk, nor an easy scramble, for the last 30m. (100 ft.) are exposed and some hard moves cannot be avoided.

Leave the hotel by the track on the west bank of the Allt Dearg Mor. Cross the foot-bridge and continue along a well-marked track towards the mountain. This path divides after the Allt Dearg Beag is joined, with the right fork going beside the river towards Coir' a' Bhasteir; your track (though un-marked on all but the latest maps) goes left across the river

34

(small bridge at present), west of the hump of Nead na h-Iolaire to Coire Riabhach. Here it keeps well above the lochan below the ridge. Skirting across this corrie it ceases to be a winding track across the heather, boulders and hummocks, and rises up to the south-east ridge by means of an easy scramble over scree and some boulders. It is very well marked and cairned all the way, though there are minor variations in the route. Once on the ridge, turn right, north-west, and continue up the crest. The route is now exposed and some of the scrambling is moderate or hard. Another way can be found a little below the ridge on the Lota Corrie side but this, too, ends in a section of hard, exposed scrambling up a rock wall.

After this narrow and airy approach, the summit makes a comfortable lunch spot with a splendid feeling of height and space and views in all directions. If you scramble a little further along the summit ridge, you can make your way through a "window" made by blocks of rock. Then the ridges begin to fall away. To the north is the Pinnacle Ridge whose serrations will have been seen on the way up as it towered above you. It requires rock climbing and no attempt should be made to descend it. To the west is the west ridge which leads down to Bealach a' Bhasteir. If you are not put off by the exposed and rather loose top section, it is inviting to scramble down here to make a round. Most of the ridge is fairly easy scrambling but low down it is guarded by the Gendarme (Policeman, occasionally called the "Tooth"). This is a large block of rock about 3m. high which bars the way on a shattered and exposed section. It is a rock climb and so are all the alternative ways down.

Unless you are a competent and equipped climber, you are therefore left with no choice on the summit but to return the way you ascended. If you keep just below the crest, make sure you do not go too far away to the right where it overlooks Lota Corrie.

Reaching the cairn on the south-east ridge marking the descent to the left, it is possible to continue along the ridge towards Sgurr Beag to find a more extensive view but return to the cairn and descend the way you came. (Time to summit, $3\frac{1}{2}$ hours. Descent $2\frac{1}{2}$ hours).

2 Bealach a'Mhaim   346m.   (1135 ft.)
Pass of the Rounded Hill.

This is not a pass over the ridge but a saddle on the track which was once the normal route between Sligachan and Glen Brittle. Today most people approach the latter by some form of transport, yet the path is in frequent use. Beside being a delightful walk in its own right, it is also the key to several of the mountains towards the northern end of the range. It opens up splendid views of peaks and corries and can form a very useful introduction to this part of the ridge.

It is well-marked all the way, though care is needed in thick mist not to follow branch tracks to the mountains and corries. It takes about $1\frac{1}{4}$ hours to walk to the top from either side: but then you have to get back.

From Glen Brittle. This is the shorter route.

Leave the Glen Brittle to Carbost road just below the steep rise and sharp bends where the road is double track. Parking is available by one of the Forestry Commission entrances but do not obstruct the gate. The path begins opposite and drops down to the small burn. Keep up and to the left here, for another track is appearing which crosses the burn lower down and leads directly down to Coire na Creiche. Follow this main route as it meanders across the moor. As it steepens, and shortly before the highest point, another track goes off between a very large triangular cairn and a small lochan. This is the normal way to Coire na Creiche, and the mountains ascended from it, when coming from Sligachan. If aiming for Bruach na Frithe, it is possible in good visibility to strike upward from here on the north-west shoulder until the ridge narrows and the main path is joined. It is a pleasant way and the views are reached earlier. However, if weather or experience are doubtful, keep on the main path until a line of cairns goes off right leading directly to Bruach na Frithe and Fionn Choire. If seeking the latter or Sgurr a' Bhasteir, in good weather it is also possible to go right of the lochan, keeping low along the sheep tracks, until the main path is reached.

From Sligachan

Though slightly longer, this is probably the more attractive way, though it would not be worth the drive round if you were staying on the other side.

A car can be left beside the road from Sligachan to Carbost where the sign says "Glen Brittle", and the drive followed towards Allt Dearg House. Avoiding the house, splash round it on the north-west; then take the path which now goes clearly up beside the burn.

If aiming for either Fionn Choire or Bruach na Frithe, keep to the main track until a large burn comes in on the right. After this a line of cairns goes diagonally off left towards the mountains. (About one hour).

If there is time it is worth walking to the top of Am Mam from which there is an excellent view.

3 Coir' a' Bhasteir

Approached by the rocky side of an impressive gorge, and girt about by the splendour of the ridges of Sgurr nan Gillean and the face of Am Basteir, this is an awesome place. Apart from some easy but exposed scrambling across the slabs, it is no more trying than a long walk and it is worth a visit for its own sake, whether it is the intention to continue to the ridge or not.

As for Sgurr nan Gillean, leave the hotel by the track on the west bank of the Allt Dearg Mor. Cross the footbridge and

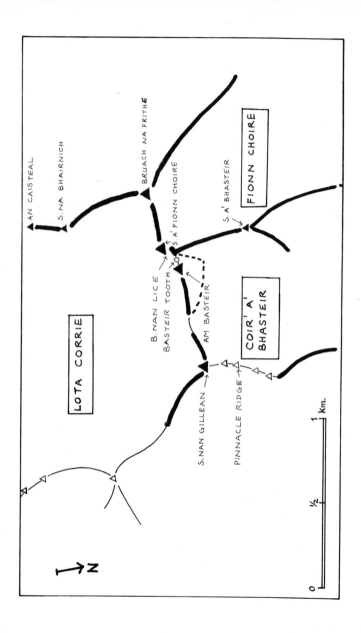

side ridges and corries	main ridge	metres	feet
	S. nan Gillean	965	3167
	B. a' Bhasteir	833	2733
(Coir' a' Bhasteir)			
	Am Basteir	936	3069
	Basteir Tooth	916	3005
	B. nan Lice → (Lota Corrie)	c885	2900
S. a' Bhasteir 900m. 2951 ft. — (Fionn Choire)			
	S. a' Fionn Choire	935	3068
	dip	c903	2964
	Bruach na Frithe	958	3143

KEY TO RIDGE DIAGRAMS

▬▬ ridge, ▲ peak, accessible by scrambling

— ridge, △ peak, only accessible by rock climbing

- - - - path which bypasses rock climb

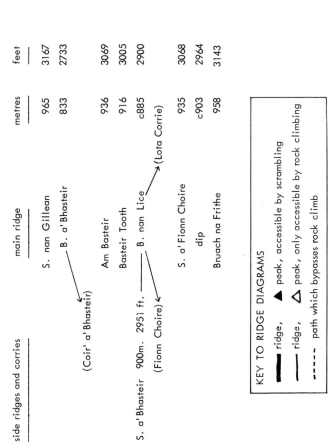

continue along the path until you reach the **Allt Dearg Beag** and another footbridge. For the corrie, do not cross the bridge but continue on the right fork beside this most attractive burn with its cataracts and clear turquoise pools. The way leads right up to the rocky chasm marking the entrance to the corrie. Behind, to the south-east, the Pinnacle Ridge frets the skyline.

At 425m. (1400 ft.) the track ascends slabs on the right, or west side, of the cleft. It is cairned and quite well-marked but is no longer an easy walk beside the stream. Though there are no difficulties, it involves a little scrambling and its posision above the gorge gives a feeling of exposure in places, especially when the slabs are wet.

Near 600m. (2000 ft.) you come into the seclusion of the corrie with its lochan. Ahead lies the wall of Am Basteir; if your destination is that peak, the west ridge of Sgurr nan Gillean or Bealach a' Bhasteir, then your route lies up scree trending a little to the left. ($2\frac{1}{2}$ hours to the bealach).

4 Bealach a'Bhasteir   833m. (2733 ft.)

From here you may admire the west ridge of Gillean, ascend Am Basteir, or go further south along the ridge by keeping under the west side of both Am Basteir and the Tooth to Bealach nan Lice. To continue along the ridge from Am Basteir summit involves rock climbing.

The bealach leads down into Lota Corrie; bald and unpleasant at the top. Should you wish to reach Lota Corrie you are advised to do it via Bealach nan Lice (Route 9).

5 Am Basteir   936m. (3069 ft.)

(Vash-tir) The Executioner, possibly from the likeness of the Tooth to a headsman's axe.

Am Basteir leads straight up from Bealach a' Bhasteir and is a natural continuation from there. When coming from the south, on reaching the Tooth you must drop down on the left or north side for nearly 150m. (500 ft.), skirting under the cliff until the bealach is reached.

The ascent to the summit is quite straightforward with easy scrambling along its narrow ridge, or an airy walk on the Lota Corrie side. Near the top there is a short descent with some 3m. (10 ft.) of exposed and moderate scrambling. The holds are there but are difficult to see with two long steps down ($\frac{3}{4}$ hour should see you up and back to the bealach).

6 Basteir Tooth   916m.   (3005 ft.)

This is one of the most dramatic rock towers in Skye; especially when climbers are seen on the Lota Corrie face. It has no possibilities for the scrambler and knowledge of this weird obelisk must be restricted to the view from below. There are also good vantage points from Sgurr a' Fionn Choire and Sgurr a' Bhasteir.

7 Sgurr a' Bhasteir   900m.   (2951 ft.)

The scramble along the ridge is easy; or walk just below the crest on a path to the summit.

This northerly spur ending in the mound of Meall Odhar gives good views, especially of Am Basteir and the Tooth. It is also a pleasant way down from the main ridge but route finding off the end needs care. There is easy scree on the east side for some distance but threading a way through cliffs at the end could be tricky and it is better to return to the nose. The descent into Fionn Choire should also keep towards the nose, dodging through many little crags. It is all scree covered and very loose but with no technical difficulties.

8 Fionn Choire

Literally "the fair corrie" and noted for its softness and greenness for a Cuillin corrie. On a fine summer's day this is indeed so, but it is possible to be blown off one's feet and bruised on its stones in bad conditions: the description "walk" is only relative. It is also known for its flowers and a number of the mountain species can easily be seen here.

To reach the corrie, come in from the Bealach a' Mhaim path (Route 2), picking up the line of cairns going towards the corrie. The way to Bruach na Frithe goes right and upwards while the way into the corrie keeps close to the north-east side of the stream. The track here begins to steepen up scree and boulders to the Bealach nan Lice; it is well marked and cairned.

9 Bealach nan Lice   c. 885m.   (2900 ft.)

(Leeka) Pass of the flat stones.

Arriving on the bealach in mist, a small knobble of rock occupies the middle before the Tooth looms up on the left, or north, end. Also on the left but before the Tooth, the small cairn for Sgurr a' Bhasteir can be seen a little away from the ridge in a northerly direction. The path to the right of the knobble goes toward Sgurr a' Fionn Choire and on to Bruach na Frithe. (Time: $2\frac{1}{2}$ hours to the bealach).

As a pass, the bealach leads to Lota Corrie and eventually to Harta Corrie; it does not lead directly to Coruisk. Walkers and climbers may descend this way but there is no track or cairns and, after an easy start down scree under the Basteir Tooth, the way over and through the slabs below is unmarked and not simple to find. At the waterfall down into Harta Corrie keep to the left, that is east, bank of the burn; this short section is cairned. Lower down a track develops on the south bank and passes the Bloody Stone; then there is the long haul down Glen Sligachan.

10 Sgurr a' Fionn Choire   935m.   (3068 ft.)

This castle of rock on the main ridge is defended on all quarters except the north where it can be bypassed altogether by a good path, or you can almost walk up it. The summit is a fine

42

vantage point, especially for the Basteir Tooth.

From the west a moderate scramble can be achieved by keeping to the ridge; if it becomes too hard it can always be turned on the north.

11 Bruach na Frithe   958m.   (3143 ft.)

(Bruach na Free) The brae of the deer forest.

This mountain is one of the few on the Cuillin ridge which can be ascended without scrambling, though it offers opportunities for this if desired. As a way to the ridge for the walker, it should not be lightly undertaken, especially in bad weather when route finding can cause problems. As a viewpoint it is widely extolled for most of the ridge can be seen.

The ascent is made from the Bealach a' Mhaim track (Route 2), then either up the north-west ridge of the mountain or into Fionn Choire and steeply up the scree at its head. Another approach takes the ridge of Sgurr a' Bhasteir (Route 7) which lies on the left, or north, of the corrie.

When ascending the north-west ridge, the crest can be followed all the way; it is often only a walk and higher up an easy scramble. There is also a path a little lower on the south-west side which is fairly well marked and only requires a little easy scrambling in a few places. This path goes off well after the crest has become a rock scramble so beware of taking a lower sheep track as soon as the rock is reached; this goes nowhere. (Time: 3 hours to summit).

For descending into Fionn Choire in a mist, the S.M.T. district guide offers a strong warning to ordinary walkers, pointing out how featureless the terrain is at 450m. (1500 ft.). It recommends descending from the summit due north until coming down into Fionn Choire, then following 330° (magnetic) until you meet a stream which should be flowing northerly and can be followed. Since that was written the track in Fionn Choire to the Bealach nan Lice has become far more clearly

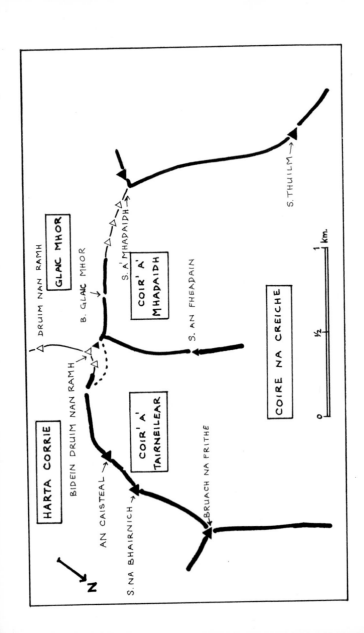

side ridges and corries	main ridge	metres	feet
	Bruach na Frithe	958	3143
	dip	845	2772
	S. na Bhairnich	861	2826
(Coir' a' Tairmeilear) ←	dip	c764	2507
	An Caisteal	830	2724
(Coir' a' Tairmeilear) ←	B.C. a' Tairmeilear	760	2494
	N. top Bidein	852	2794
	dip	c823	2700
	Bidein Druim nan Ramh	869	2850
	dip	c823	2700
S. an Fheadain c687m. 2253 ft.—W. top Bidein	W. top Bidein	847	2779
	B. na Glaic Mhor	760 (Glaic Mhor)	2492
(Coir' a' Mhadaidh) ←	N.E. top S. a' Mhadaidh	896	2939
	dip	871	2858
	top (2)	887	2910
	dip	866	2840
	top (3)	894	2934
	dip	860	2820
S. Thuilm 879m. 2885 ft. —— S. a' Mhadaidh (summit)	S. a' Mhadaidh (summit)	918	3012
dip 747m. 2452 ft.			

marked so the essential exercise is to get safely back to this bealach.

The compass can be unreliable here, as on all peaks, but if you descend well away from the top and the triangulation point, and take several readings, you ought to be able to get a rough idea of the easterly direction to take to be sure of the path which leads to the bealach. If in doubt, trend more north than south of east. To miss the path on the north means rough going and having to avoid some rocks; to miss it south of east would mean encountering difficulties.

Shortly after the summit the way becomes more obvious and soon develops into a path. Sgurr a' Fionn Choire is bypassed and the bealach is recognised by a knobble of rock. A descent is seen going down into Lota Corrie on the right and the cairns of the Fionn Choire track on the left, or west, side. If you meet the Tooth looming out of the mist, you have gone too far.

12 Sgurr na Bhairnich   861m.   (2826 ft.)

The Limpet.

From Bruach na Frithe the ridge goes south for nearly one km., mainly downwards, to the odd shaped lump of Sgurr na Bhairnich. By Cuillin standards it is easy but there are a couple of moderate bits.

From the summit of Bruach na Frithe, go south and slightly right and the line of wear will be seen. Very soon there is a short slab with an awkward long step across, but it is not really hard. The rest is exposed walking until the rise to the summit where there is a short, moderate, but not exposed, scramble to the top.

Return can be made to Bruach na Frithe or the ridge continued to the deep gash. The latter is easy but has some feeling of exposure in descending the scree covered ledges. It is best to keep to the nose. A gully with red-brown rock will be crossed a little below the crest on the left. It is tempting on the west side but this has problems at the bottom so it should not be followed. Shortly afterwards, descend into the correct (grey) gully where 300m. (1000 ft.) of scree leads down into Coir' a' Tairneilear.

13 Coire na Creiche

"Corrie of the Spoil", named after a battle between the Macdonalds and the Macleods in 1601.

The corrie is bounded to the north by the north-west ridge of Bruach na Frithe, and on the south by Sgurr Thuilm. Along its north-western side runs the Bealach a' Mhaim path from Glen Brittle to Sligachan. It is generally a flat and boggy corrie but it contains the Allt Coir' a' Mhadaidh which becomes the River Brittle. With its series of deep blue pools (the Fairy Pools), white cascades and rock arches, it is most attractive and, if not visited on the way to the ridge, it affords a delightful evening walk.

The upper part of the corrie is divided by the peak of Sgurr an Fheadain, with its famous Waterpipe Gully, into two upper corries. That to the left, or north, of the buttress is properly Coir' a' Tairneilear but older books and maps refer to it as Coir' a' Mhadaidh. The latter title belongs more properly to the right hand, or more southern, corrie which lies under the peak of that name, though this was formerly known as Coir' a' Tairneilear.

14 Coir' a' Tairneilear

The Thunderer

There are two approaches.

a. From the Bealach a' Mhaim. Between the south-west end of the lochan and the high triangular cairn a well marked line leads off south-west to become a sheep track with a few cairns as it traverses under Bruach na Frithe.

b. From Glen Brittle. A car can be parked as for the Bealach a' Mhaim. Then the shortest route is via the left, or north, bank of the Allt coir' a' Mhadaidh.

After the entrance to the corrie the track rises and the ground becomes rougher. It is clearly cairned but there are signs that it is becoming overmarked. The main line of cairns stays fairly close to the left hand side of the burn and the temptation to make for high ground should be resisted. A stream comes from the left, over slabs, at about 400m. (1300 ft.) which, like many streams in Skye, can rise quickly and cause crossing problems after a downpour, but it is best to stick to the cairned line.

The corrie flattens somewhat around 425m. (1350 ft.) and here the very long scree shoot arrives from the north end of An Caisteal on the left, while the track leads up through the cliffs and boulders to another scree straight ahead. Follow this scree for 30 to 60m. (100 to 200 ft.) until a small cairn indicates the way to the right. Cairns, again increasing, mark the way through the slabs until the main scree coming down from the bealach between An Caisteal and Bidein Druim nan Ramh is reached.

The bealach is not a pass to Coruisk but leads down into Harta Corrie. It is best approached from the Bidein end of the dip and it has no problems except for loose, little used scree and it is unmarked.

15 Coire'a' Mhadaidh

Approaches as for Coir' a' Tairneilear.

A track passes under the Waterpipe Gully; from this either rise directly to gain the corrie or continue along the traversing path under some more cliffs until the cairns lead up a gully on the left hand side of the burn.

Once in the main corrie, follow the left hand (true right or north) bank of the burn. The path is marked on the map but it is not very distinct on the ground. When the headwall of smooth rock cut by three gullies rises ahead, you have arrived.

To reach Bealach Glaic Mhor (Route 19) go straight up scree to the left toward the West peak of Bidein Druim nan Ramh. Formerly the advice was to avoid this rough, unstable scree but it is being used more often now and it is not too bad except where it gets thin and rocky at the top. However, route finding in mist remains a problem so perhaps it is best left for good conditions.

If your goal is only the corrie itself, and a very worthwhile corrie this is, then before the headwall of rock, take to the low angled slabs on the right and go across to admire the imposing cliffs of Sgurr a' Mhadaidh. There is no easy route to the ridge from here.

16 Sgurr an Fheadain   687m.   (2253 ft.)

(Ait-yan) Peak of the Waterpipe.

This ridge, dividing the two arms of Coire na Creiche, terminates in the great rock buttress which is split by the famous Waterpipe Gully. The gully itself is a serious rock climb, yet a way to the top can be found by the scrambler which is only moderate, though quite exposed. It presents a fine approach to the ridge on either side of Bidein Druim nan Ramh, or to the Bealach na Glaic Mhor.

To reach the bottom of the buttress use any of the approach ways described under Coire na Creiche (Route 13). Keeping to the left of the lowest point, ways up may be picked over the slabs until the angle steepens and the crest of the ridge is gained. There are no real difficulties if a good line is taken but it is not a mere walk. The scramble up the crest is easy but with a fine sense of exposure and some rotten rock.

From the summit go down on the right, or south, side to a dip; then along the relatively level ridge. The scrambling here is all easy but can always be turned on the right.

In descent, keep to the scree at the end of the level section

An Caisteal. Easy 'grey' gully on the left.

rather than go down the nose and the slabs at the bottom. This scree goes down easily into Coir' a' Tairneilear but you have to watch for some cliffs low down, where you should keep to the left.

Where the ridge meets the main mountain can be confusing in poor visibility and the reader may find the notes on Bealach na Glaic Mhor useful (Route 19). (Ascent time: 1 hour up the nose, $\frac{1}{2}$ hour along the ridge).

17 An Caisteal 830m. (2724 ft.)

The Castle.

This section of the ridge lies between Sgurr na Bhairnich and Bidein Druim nan Ramh. Though it is not marked on the O. S. map it is a fine looking mountain which really does resemble a castle as it dominates Coir' a' Tairneilear. It is regarded by the pundits as "easy" but it is loose, exposed, and the descent from the north end is hard. It is one of the few places on the ridge where care is required in finding the route.

It can be approached from the north from Bruach na Frithe, over Sgurr na Bhairnich. It would be possible to gain the north end from Coir' a' Tairneilear by the long scree to the gash between Bhairnich and An Caisteal but this would be exceedingly laborious as a way up and is better in descent. From the south-west you can either come over Sgurr an Fheadain (Route 16) and under the cliffs of Bidein Druim nan Ramh, or continue up Coir' a' Tairneilear to the bealach.

Leaving this (southern) bealach scramble over a rock lump. The standard is about moderate but there is a hard move for those with limited reach. It can be avoided by an airy traverse on the east side or, by a short descent to easier ground, can be avoided altogether on the west. It is then a walk until the ridge narrows and becomes exposed and decidedly shattered and loose in places. The actual scrambling is easy to the summit with two awkward sections. In one, red arrows on the rock go round on the west but it is easier to keep to the crest where there is some sign of wear. In the other, a gash splits the ridge; either jump across or go about $2\frac{1}{2}$m. (8 ft.) down a slab on the east.

After the summit it is important not to keep to the ridge until it ends in a dramatic drop into Harta Corrie. A steep scree "path" - loose and impressive - goes off to the west and leads down under a wall then across some slabs to the top of the final wall down to the gully. This wall is steep and exposed but all the holds are there and it proves a very pleasant, moderate scramble, easier at the top than the bottom which is hard. It is probably easier from north to south.

To the north the dip between An Caisteal and Sgurr na Bhairnich presents a deep gash some 60m. (200 ft.) lower than the summit of the former. Once down, there is a long 300m. (1000 ft.) but easy scree run into Coir' a' Tairneilear. Alternatively, if not discouraged by An Caisteal, you can continue over Sgurr na Bhairnich to Bruach na Frithe and go down from there.

At the southern end of An Caisteal you can descend from the dip before Bidein Druim nan Ramh into Coir' a' Tairneilear, or go over Sgurr an Fheadain.

18 Bidein Druim nan Ramh   Central Peak 869m. (2850 ft.)
(Bidyan Drim nan Rahv) Pinnacle of the Ridge of Oars.

This mountain whose three peaks form a triangle on the ridge has a varied silhouette. The summit or central peak is usually masked, or dwarfed into insignificance, when seen from Coire na Creiche, but it appears as a huge fortress when seen from the Bealach na Glaic Mhor. From the summit the long ridge of the Druim nan Ramh stretches down to divide Coruisk and Harta Corrie.

The traverse of the three peaks contains rock climbing and should not be attempted by the scrambler. You can, however,

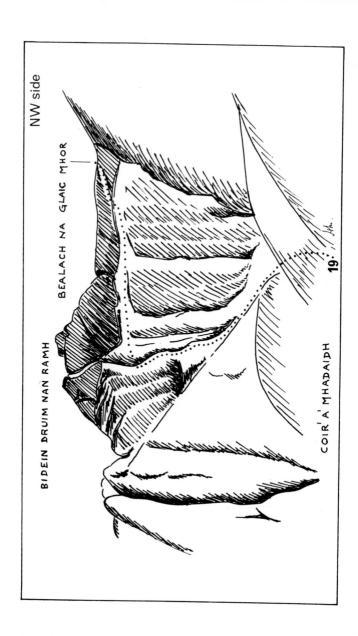

NW side

BIDEIN DRUIM NAN RAMH

BEALACH NA GLAIC MHOR

COIR' A' MHADAIDH

19.

traverse scree under the face on the west side. It involves a certain amount of descent and reascent but it provides a way from the head of Coir' a' Tairneilear to Bealach na Glaic Mhor.

19 Bealach na Glaic Mhor   760m.   (2492 ft.)

(Glas Vore) Pass of the Great Hollow.

This is one of the main passes to Coruisk but its position away from huts, hostels and campsites, together with its distance from Coruisk, means it is not often used. It is also confusing in mist on both sides of the ridge.

To reach this bealach the easiest way is via Coir' a' Tairneilear (Route 14) until arriving on the screes at a height a little below the bottom of the cliff of Bidein Druim nan Ramh. In mist it could be wiser to go all the way to the bealach between Bidein and An Caisteal ($2\frac{1}{2}$ hours) then work over, down and round the bottom of the cliff. Struggle up the scree under the West Peak of Bidein until you meet the ridge. From there follow the scratches and the odd cairn until you reach the wide, flat area of the bealach.

A second and more exciting way, if one is able and not carrying a load, is via Sgurr an Fheadain (Route 16).

A third approach is by Coir' a' Mhadaidh (Route 15). From the top of this scree you have to traverse right, or south, below some small crags at about 700m. (2300 ft.); it is neither cairned nor is there much sign of wear. In descent keep high up under the crags, avoiding a gully which is marked at the top with a cairn: it is very loose.

There are two branches to the pass into Coruisk. The way down is straightforward; more easily made by the northern one. Ascent can be difficult in mist. Keep to the main river bed, forking right at the junction, until it ends. The best route then makes for the southern branch and keeps left of the scree on rock and grass.

Coir' an Dorus from the ridge of Sgurr Thuilm leading to Sgurr a'Mhadaidh. The scree gully of An Dorus is the lowest point on the skyline and the peak of Sgurr a'Ghreadaidh with its 'wart' can be seen on the right.

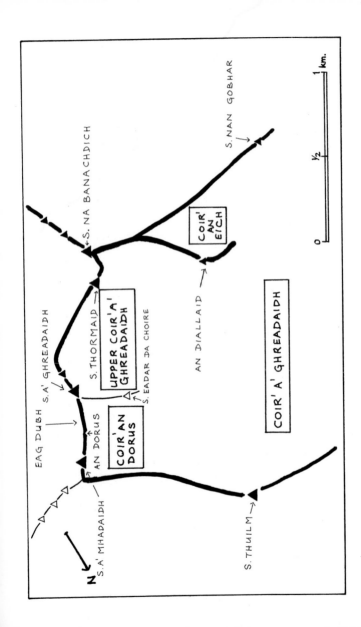

side ridges and corries	main ridge	metres	feet
S. Thuilm 879m. 2885 ft. ——	S. a' Mhadaidh	918	3012
dip 747m. 2452 ft.	An Dorus	847	2779
(Coir' an Dorus) →			
	Eag Dubh	c884	2900
S. Eadar da Choire ——	S. a' Ghreadaidh	973	3192
809m. 2655 ft.	dip	955	3133
	South top	970	3181
	dip	849	2784
	Three Teeth	c902	2950
	dip	c892	2925
	S. Thormaid	927	3034
	dip	888	2914
(Coir' an Eich) →			
S. nan Gobhar ——	S. na Banachdich	965	3166
631m. 2069 ft.			

20 Coir'a' Ghreadaidh

This is the main corrie at the foot of Sgurr a' Ghreadaidh and leads to three upper corries. These are Coir' an Dorus in the north under Sgurr Thuilm; upper Coir' a' Ghreadaidh under the main face of the mountain; and Coir' an Eich out to the south between An Diallaid and Sgurr nan Gobhar.

A well-defined path rises gradually beside the Allt a' Choire Ghreadaidh from the Youth Hostel. After half an hour or so the burn falls over a series of slabs for about 100m. (300 ft.). The track is on the right but it ceases at the top with a large cairn. Here the corrie floor flattens and, though the boulders are smaller than in many other corries, it has a wild and desolate air. As the ground rises again the corrie is split by the spur of Sgurr Eadar da Choire (the peak between the corries) which comes down in a cascade of rotten rock from about 60m. (200 ft.) below the North summit of Sgurr a' Ghreadaidh. It is loose and not recommended as a way to the top.

21 Sgurr Thuilm   879m.   (2885 ft.)

(Hulim) Peak of Tulm.

The massive end of Sgurr Thuilm, so noticeable on the drive into Glen Brittle, gives a misleading impression, though when toiling up its screes this seems justified. It also has a very pleasant summit ridge which is easy, and an exhilarating but sharp rise connecting it to the main ridge at Sgurr a' Mhadaidh.

The best approach is from the Youth Hostel and along the Allt a' Choire Ghreadaidh until it flows over a series of slabs. Here cross over to the north side and, after rising up beside the slabs, take the left of two streams to reach the crags at about 400m. (1300 ft.). Ascent can be made in many places; the easiest misses the first triangular crag seen as you come towards the corrie and goes up scree beside a series of outcrops beginning on the right. When higher than the crags, trend east up scree to join the ridge just before the summit. (Time:

hostel to summit of Sgurr Thuilm, 2¼ hours).

The ridge is rarely more than a walk, though quite exposed, until it rises against the side of Sgurr a' Mhadaidh. This contains sections which are both exposed and hard. It is a fine scramble for those with the nerve and ability but otherwise it should not be attempted.

There is a cairn just before the rise begins. From here escape back into the corrie can be made down an easy rake on the south. The choice then is either to return to the Allt a' Choire Ghreadaidh or to traverse under one set of cliffs, then rising across scree and through other cliffs to An Dorus. It is not tracked but it is not difficult to find the way in good visibility.

If the conditions are good and you consider you have the experience to ascend the ridge, scramble along until the rock steepens. In front of you, split by the huge cleft of Deep Gash Gully, the ridge to Sgurr a' Mhadaidh rises impressively. Immediately ahead there are two ribs; the route lies up the left of these, though it is easier at the beginning to keep just below the crest on the right. You should not keep on this side too long but work round to the left for a short distance. There are several places where the scrambling is hard and the situation exposed. As the ridge levels out there is a cairn which marks the top of Foxes Rake: BEWARE, this is not an easy way down. There is a note on the Rake for climbers in the appendix.

22 An Dorus   847m.   (2779 ft.)

The Door.

From Route 20 take the left hand, or northerly, branch of the stream (there are two main streams joining here in spite of the map) and keep to the right hand side. Though there are a few scattered cairns it is best to follow the burn in mist. Shortly you rise over a few slabs while the water pours down a small ravine beside them. Then the corrie flattens once more and the stream, now quite small, divides. The left branch comes down another small rock ravine but you follow the right hand branch which soon disappears. You find yourself in a boulder and scree filled gully which looks as if it once held a larger burn. Here the track is clearly marked and cairned. In good visibility make for the left hand skyline cleft, which is An Dorus. In mist it will be noticed that the cairns give out when some larger boulders and slabs appear ahead. The natural line of scree seems to go straight up but this leads to the right hand cleft of the Eag Dubh (Black Notch, 884m., 2900 ft.). Where the cairns disappear, track up and slightly left, so missing the slabs, and soon the worn scree descending from An Dorus will be apparent. (Time: Hostel to An Dorus 2½ hours).

As an alternative excursion it is worthwhile following the right hand stream below Sgurr Eadar da Choire to enter the even more remote upper Coir' a' Ghreadaidh. There is rock climbing here but no easy route to the ridge. To reach the upper corrie it is best to start by scrambling up slabs on the left of the stream and higher up to move over to the other bank. There is no lochan in this corrie, no cairns and consequently it is a difficult place to negotiate in mist.

23 Sgurr a'Mhadaidh   918m.   (3012 ft.)

(Vha-ty) The Foxes Peak.

This mountain lies between Bealach na Glaic Mhor and the pass of An Dorus. Its one km. ridge runs north-east to south-west over four tops, of which the south-west is the highest. The traverse of the ridge includes rock climbing but, luckily for the scrambler, the main top can be reached fairly easily from the south.

The usual way up is through Coir' a' Ghreadaidh from the Youth Hostel, then up Coire an Dorus to the scree gully of An

Dorus (Route 22). From An Dorus take the ridge to the left, or north. A short 2m. (6 ft.) rock wall immediately above the gap is moderate but not exposed; some prefer the more exposed loose channel overlooking the Coruisk side. After that the scrambling is easy and almost everything can be avoided on the west side though this spoils the fun. The summit is the near side of a tilted slab with a crack running along it. With hands on the top and feet in the crack it is impressive yet easy to cross; it too can be avoided on the west. (Time: under $\frac{1}{2}$ hour from An Dorus).

It is possible to continue along the ridge for a little until you see the rock dipping towards the ridge of Thuilm. Unless you intend to descend it, you are advised not to continue for, though a way can be made down to the corrie, it consists of scree ledges which are loose and dangerous. View the rest of the ridge of Sgurr a' Mhadaidh, absorb the prospect of Coruisk - and return the way you came. In mist it might be wiser not to go beyond the summit as it is a complex area and care is needed not to take the wrong ridge.

To make a round of Thuilm, Mhadaidh, Ghreadaidh, Thormaid and Banachdich is a splendid expedition but it is long, exposed and hard in places with no escape after An Dorus.

24 Sgurr a'Ghreadaidh   973m.   (3192 ft.)
(Gret-a)   Peak of Thrashings, or Mighty Winds, or Clear Waters.

The traverse of this part of the ridge is one of the best sections for the scrambler. It is narrow and often dramatic; on the whole the rock is sound and the holds good, so there is exposure but with a fair sense of security. The general scrambling standard is moderate though there are one or two places which are hard if taken direct. Because the ridge is narrow, route finding is straightforward.

For the north end, approach from An Dorus. The initial

climb out of the An Dorus gap is up a 6m. (20 ft.) wall of moderate scrambling with the holds all there. Then the ridge becomes little more than a walk for a while. Shortly you have to cross the impressive gash of Eag Dubh (Black Notch, 884m., 2900 ft.). Tackle it by following the scratch marks down on the Coruisk side, then rejoin the ridge beyond the gap by a scramble, also on that side. You then arrive at one of those curious lumps of rock which occur on the Cuillin: this is often referred to as the "wart". Go up on to it or avoid it on the west. There is no real problem in finding the route if you keep close to the wart. Reference is sometimes made to the spur of Sgurr Eadar da Choire but it is much lower and there is little danger of straying off route.

After the wart the ridge narrows and the interesting bits occur. On this section there are two summits, both cairned, the North one (973m., 3192 ft.) almost immediately. Going down the ridge from the North Top a rib of rock provides a short, interesting scramble. It is exposed but there are large ledges for the feet, though those with limited reach may find them far apart. After the South summit (970m., 3181 ft.) the ridge remains narrow; it is easier but very broken and loose. High up there is another slabby rib which is also exposed with a long, awkward step down. The rest of the way is easy.

At the dip between Ghreadaidh and Thormaid, which is recognisable by a circle of rocks, there is a possible way down to the corrie below but it is loose, unpleasant and no place for the scrambler. By far the best retreat from here is to continue over Thormaid.

25 Sgurr Thormaid   927m.   (3040 ft.)

(Har-a-mich) Norman's Peak, after Professor Norman Collie.

This small but dramatic peak lies inevitably on the ridge between Sgurr a' Ghreadaidh and Sgurr na Banachdich. Approaching from Ghreadaidh the scrambler first arrives at the

Three Teeth. There is a traverse path on the west side which goes off near the bealach. Either take this from the start or go up and over the first of the teeth, which is very easy. The second tooth can be climbed or avoided: it is easy in ascent but less so coming down. Likewise the third, which is definitely the hardest, but can also be avoided.

The route then lies up a tilted slab ahead which is Thormaid. It is best taken directly up the crest which is not hard. Alternatively, a path leads round on the Coruisk side to finish by mounting up the slab. It is an airy peak but not difficult. Easy scrambling takes you down to the col with various avoidances available on the west.

There is a bealach between Thormaid and Banachdich which has three knobbles or little pinnacles on it, all very small and easy to cross if taken directly. The descent from this bealach into Coir' a' Ghreadaidh is loose and dangerous. The only quick and safe way down is to make the 75m. (250 ft.) of height to the top of Sgurr na Banachdich and descend Coir' an Eich. (Time: An Dorus to the summit of Banachdich, $1\frac{1}{2}$-2 hours, but allow ample time as there is no easy escape).

26 Coir'an Eich

The corrie of horses.

This southern portion of Coir' a' Ghreadaidh is an easy scree bowl leading up to the junction of the spur of Sgurr nan Gobhar and the scree slope running up to the summit of Sgurr na Banachdich. It is the simplest way to reach Banachdich as it is merely a scree slog. It is hardly recommended as a way up but it is a quick and easy way off the ridge. In either direction you can use part of the ridge of An Diallaid (The Saddle) in good visibility, but keep to the Coir' an Eich side as there is a rock face on the other.

From the keel of the summit of Sgurr na Banachdich the cliffs plunge precipitously north and east. The ridge to Sgurr

Thormaid drops down very sharply in a northerly direction, passing rectangular blocks of brown rocks on your left in descent. Even further to your left, that is in a westerly direction, the cairns mark the way down for both Sgurr nan Gobhar and Coir' an Eich. The cairns all go in the same general direction, though this is yet another place where senseless cairn-building only complicates matters. If aiming for Coir' an Eich, keep to the right hand line of these, passing a rock knobble on your right or north-west. When the burn is picked up it is easier, though not essential, in mist to keep to its right, or north, side.

27 Sgurr nan Gobhar   631m.   (2069 ft.)

(Goar) The Goat's Peak.

This attractive ridge spur forms an enjoyable way to the summit of Sgurr na Banachdich or descent from it. The ascent is across the moor from Glen Brittle and up the scree; the easiest way, up or down, is via the south-west shoulder that runs up from above the Eas Mor. The scree is laborious and some of the little crags have to be climbed or avoided but the ridge can be reached in under an hour from the grass and heather.

In descent, care is needed to avoid the crags and it is best to set off for the south-west, keeping to the south side of the gully. This gully is full of rotten rock and scree, making it awkward to enter, though the climb down it is simple. Much time can be wasted finding a way down on its north side.

The ridge itself is pleasant, easy scrambling with one section high up that is moderate if taken direct. As the spur meets the mountain, cairns lead upward to the main top of Banachdich. It is possibly the easiest way to reach the main ridge: it is certainly the shortest. ($2\frac{1}{2}$ hours).

Sgurr Dearg with the Inaccessible Pinnacle and An Stac. Beyond is Sgurr na Banachdich.

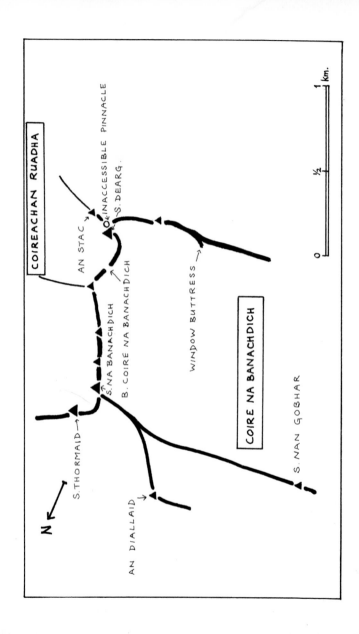

side ridges and corries	main ridge	metres	feet
S. nan Gobhar 631m. 2069 ft. ——— S. na Banachdich		965	3166
	dip	c917	3010
	top (2)	942	3089
	dip	908	2979
	top (3)	921	3023
	dip	867	2845
	top (4)	880	2887
	B.C. na Banachdich	851	2791
	→(Coireachan Ruadha)		
(Coire na Banachdich)			
west ridge 929m. 3049 ft.——— S. Dearg		978	3209

28 Coire na Banachdich

For a long time this corrie had a bad reputation especially in mist. It is composed of rock terraces, slabs and cliffs and it is still possible to get into difficulties here but it is now well marked and with care no problem should arise.

From Glen Brittle House a path goes up beside the burn, initially on the south side. The track goes into the corrie but watch that you do not go off right on the more beaten way that goes to Coire Lagan. When the corrie begins to steepen, this route bears right and up the side of Sgurr Dearg for a time.

From the campsite a track is being worn across the moor to the shoulder which comes down from Sgurr Dearg. After you have begun to rise up the lower part of the shoulder, at about 350m. (1200 ft.), a cairn marks a well defined path which traverses round the south side of the corrie to a prominent rock buttress called Window Buttress, having a noticeable "window" high up. There is a tempting gully in this buttress but it does not lead anywhere except as a descent from rock climbs. When approaching the buttress, the path goes across the scree. At the first fork keep high; the lower path loses height though it does avoid an easy rock slab. At the second fork keep low, for the upper path only leads to the gully. Traverse round the buttress then across boulders below the cliffs, passing a cairn or two, to join an open rake rising in the slabs ahead. Another line of cairns goes off at a higher level behind the buttress but this leads over slabby rock and can be unpleasant in the wet.

At the rake the two recommended routes meet. The line of cairns comes up from the corrie bottom and a clear way continues up the rake. At the top the main line traverses left across the top of the corrie to the bealach. Another line of cairns goes straight up a scree gully, then scree to the summit of Sgurr Dearg. If both ascending and descending the mountain by this corrie, it is better to go to the bealach on the way up

W side

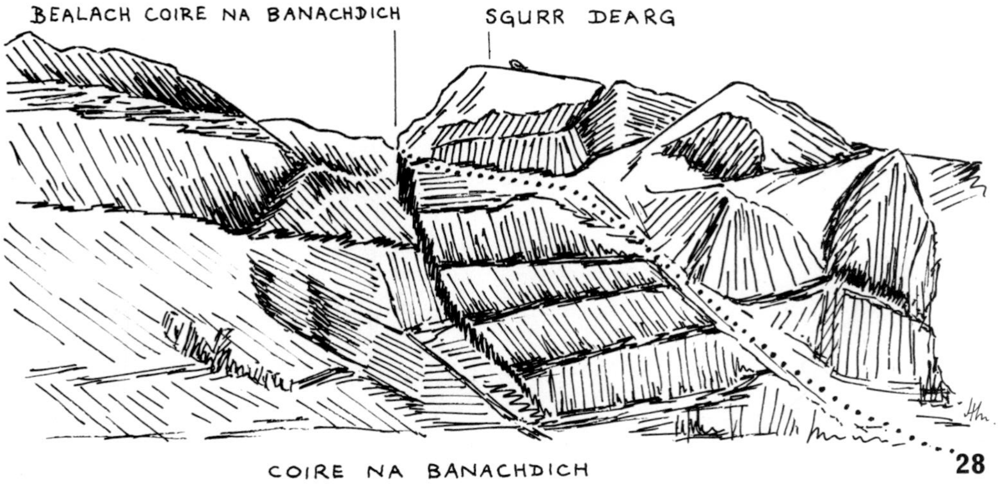

BEALACH COIRE NA BANACHDICH

SGURR DEARG

COIRE NA BANACHDICH

28

and descend more directly. A word of caution when coming down from this summit in mist. Far too many cairns have been scattered across the scree at this point and it is often difficult to know which line is being followed down. One very prominent cairn north of the summit is in the general line but keep it on your right for if followed too exactly it leads to the top of a scree gully which ends in a cliff overlooking Coruisk.

Bealach Coire na Banachdich is one of the quickest and easiest routes over the ridge to Coruisk. There is a knobble of rock on the top of the pass and descents, east and west, can be made either side of it. (Time: To the bealach from Glen Brittle, $2\frac{1}{2}$ hours. Descent, $1\frac{1}{2}$ hours).

29 Sgurr na Banachdich   965m.   (3166 ft.)
Smallpox Peak or Milkmaids Peak (meaning disputed)

Banachdich summit is one of the easiest and most accessible on the ridge. It can be reached by toiling up the Coir' an Eich scree (that will probably take 2-3 hours), or more interestingly, by the ridge of Sgurr nan Gobhar. For descent in mist, see notes on Coir' an Eich (Route 26). It is about the only Cuillin summit where the compass is reliable, though there are bad deflections on the other tops of its ridge.

To approach from Bealach Coire na Banachdich you must traverse its ridge which, though classed as "easy" for the climber, is often found to have difficulties for others. The crest is dramatically narrow and mainly very shattered. It has four tops which divide into three sections as seen from Glen Brittle. The highest point is at the northerly end, "Summit". After a dip there is the difficult section, "Sensations", after Mr. Poucher's comment on it. The final two tops which run together as seen from below, "Salvation", is mainly a walk.

The second, or difficult, section is on sounder rock but the scramble up, slightly on the west side of the north end, is hard

70

scrambling. After that it is mainly an exposed walk except for the descent of a rib which has enormous footholds but great exposure too. It is then easy scrambling onwards and finally down a wall on the west. Coming from the south, in ascent you have to notice that the way goes up this wall; an adjoining traverse path could take you further and so miss this top altogether. From either end you can take this lower traversing path which avoids the ridge; but when last seen it still consisted of a way over ledges covered with ball-bearings of scree with the side of the mountain stretching below. Some prefer this type of terrain.

Along much of the ridge it looks from above as if a way can be made down to Coire na Banachdich but it is not the easy descent it looks and is dangerous. The upper part consists of these same loose scree ledges; below are cliffs and slabs. Descent is far easier and safer at either end of the Banachdich ridge.

30 Sgurr Dearg (cairn) 978m. (3209 ft.)

(Jerrack) The Red Peak.

Sgurr Dearg must be one of the most frequently visited tops of the Cuillin. It is close to Glen Brittle, easy of access and gives superb views of the ridge.

From Bealach Coire na Banachdich it is only a scree slog up beside the multitude of cairns. A finer approach is by way of the west shoulder which mixes scree ascent, easy scrambling, and one section of fairly exposed moderate scrambling. From the campsite this route shows a head of rock which is not the summit, and which has the Window Buttress clearly visible low down on the Coire na Banachdich side.

To go up this way, cross the moor, either from Glen Brittle House or the campsite, by one of the tracks leading that way, then follow another track which makes off towards the shoulder. Take care not to follow the traverse path round to Window

Buttress but the upward route and you will find yourself scrambling up the broken dyke on the first steep rise. The course is clearly marked, though when the rocks are reached later on, the cairned ways are many and various. On the whole the scrambling is more interesting nearer the crest and more a walk on loose scree the nearer one is to the Lagan side.

After surmounting this area of broken rocks the ridge narrows for a short scramble that is no harder than that over which you have come but is much more exposed. The way ahead is obvious and soon you are walking to the summit, dramatically aloft, with magnificent views all round.

To your right, or south-east, is the weird shape of the Inaccessible Pinnacle (986m., 3234 ft.), its steep, awkward West Ridge (Diff.) nearer to you, and at the other end the long, easier East Ridge (Mod.) by which it was first ascended in 1881. Though the East Ridge is not hard, it is a rock climb and very exposed.

Beyond the Pinnacle in the distance, Blaven stands majestically aloof from its kindred gabbro peaks. Turning further south, there is the splendid amphitheatre of rock which surrounds Coire Lagan. Left to right: Mhic Coinnich, Thearlaich, Alasdair, Sgumain and the cliffs of Sron na Ciche.

The descent of Dearg can be by the way you came, or down into Coire na Banachdich (in mist, see Route 28), or down into Coire Lagan. For the latter, descend the scree covered slabs immediately below the right, or west, side of the Pinnacle. It is not, perhaps, the most comfortable of descents but it does not get any worse than the rough ground near the top.

At the foot of the East Ridge of the Pinnacle a traverse can be made out to the summit of An Stac (953m., 3125 ft. The Stack). This is merely an easy scramble and it hardly takes you out of your way. The ridge of An Stac continues down to Bealach Coire Lagan but it is classed as a rock climb; on account of the exposure, steepness and extreme looseness of the rock rather than the technical difficulties encountered. You return by the way you came. Keep close to the wall of the Pinnacle and An Stac because the tempting scree in the middle ends over the cliffs below. A cairn marks a place where you scramble up and away from the scree round an obvious corner to your left; it is all well marked. Continue in this direction until there is a choice of traversing along to Bealach Coire Lagan or making a quick descent of the An Stac screes, to the lochan in upper Coire Lagan. (Descent from the bealach to Glen Brittle House, about $1\frac{1}{2}$ hours).

31 Coire Lagan

Coire Lagan must have seen more feet than any other corrie in the Cuillin. Evidence of this is apparent in the massive tracks across the peat, in the quantity of litter, and the fact that only on a wild, wet day have you a hope of being alone there in summer.

The lower corrie is bounded by the face of Sron na Ciche which is one of the best and most varied of all cliffs in Britain for the rock climber. Nearly 300m. (1000 ft.) at its highest, and one km. wide, it contains climbs of all standards and types so that on a warm afternoon the Sron will be festooned with ropes and brightly coloured figures as decorated as a Christmas tree.

The upper corrie forms the approach to Sgurr Alasdair, and all who can, if the weather is fine, test themselves against the highest peak of the range in the manner of Ben Nevis, Snowdon and Scafell Pike. Others, too, who would never attempt a mountain and who really come to look at the Glen Brittle beach, feel the lure of the peaks and struggle across moor, mud and boulder to gain a closer view.

With its ice-ground boiler plates of brown gabbro and its acres of light grey basalt scree, it can be an impressive place but you have to be there early or very late indeed if the silence

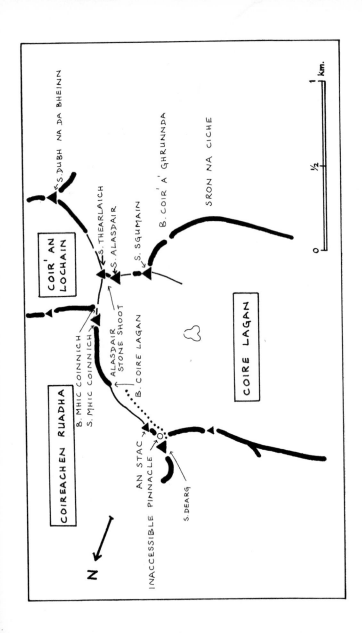

side ridges and corries	main ridge	metres	feet
west ridge 929m. 3049 ft. ——	S. Dearg	978	3209
	dip	c968	3175
	Inaccessible Pinnacle	986	3234
	dip	c942	3090
	An Stac	953	3125
	B. Coire Lagan	820	2690
(Coire Lagan) ←			
	gash	804	2639
	S. Mhic Coinnich	948	3111
	B. Mhic Coinnich	892	2928
	→(Coir' an Lochain)		
(Coire Lagan) ←			
	S. Thearlaich	978	3208

is not to be perpetually broken by the calls of climbers, the shouts of those who cannot bear silence and the constant rumble of the Alasdair scree being worn down by countless boots.

To reach the corrie from the campsite, go over the stile behind the toilets and straight up the track across the moor. When you reach the burn, do not cross it immediately but turn up left beside it. This path shortly also crosses the burn and continues upward. It is a wide scar in the peat and there is no possibility of missing the way except that you must avoid tracks going off diagonally right and down towards Sron na Ciche.

If coming from Glen Brittle House, the route is also well marked along the south side of the Eas Mor and keeping to the upper side of Loch an Fhir-bhallaich. Again beware of the right-hand branch which leads to Sron na Ciche. Should you not come in this way or do not have the time to linger, the waterfall of the Eas Mor (Big Waterfall) is well worth an evening visit, especially on one of those glorious Skye evenings which arrive tantalisingly after a day of heavy rain and thick mist. Loch an Fhir-bhallaich, too, has its charm. Red-throated Diver sometimes visit it, although it has probably become too popular for them to nest. You can also swim if you feel hardy enough.

But to return to Coire Lagan. The obvious cairned path goes all the way to the loch at 556m. (1845 ft.) and for many this is far enough. At the far end of the loch you will notice the trail going right to the Great Stone Shoot for the ascent of Sgurr Alasdair. Ahead lies the curious wedge shape of Sgurr Mhic Coinnich with its steep south end "capped by a kettle-lid", as one climber put it. Then, to its left, the nick in the skyline which is not the bealach, and left of that the true Bealach Coire Lagan. Further left still are the monstrous shapes of An Stac and the Inaccessible Pinnacle. The track continues and leads to the vast area of scree below them. If you have a stout heart, stout boots, and no opportunity to go any other way, you may toil up these screes, then scramble right up to the bealach which has very good views. There is nothing to stop you toiling even further up beside An Stac and the Inaccessible Pinnacle (see notes on descent, Route 30) but these ways are preferable in descent.

Bealach Coire Lagan is technically a pass. Though it is easy enough on the Lagan side the descent into Coruisk is difficult, loose and best left alone. It takes about 2 hours to get to the pass and just over an hour to get down.

32 Sgurr Mhic Coinnich   948m.   (3111 ft.)

Mackenzie's Peak after John Mackenzie the guide who accompanied the pioneers, especially Professor Norman Collie, when the first climbing routes were ascended.

This is a peak for the experienced scrambler with a good head for heights. Its final section is perhaps the sharpest in the Cuillin with quite spectacular drops on both sides. The only approach to the summit is from Bealach Coire Lagan, and to this you must return.

From the bealach, descend slightly on the Lagan side to avoid the deep cleft and from there the scratch marks go upwards, again more on the Lagan side. The ridge can be divided into three parts and this first section contains some very enjoyable scrambling on sound rock; some of it can be technically quite hard but not very exposed. Follow the well worn route to attain the crest as soon as possible. The middle section is mainly a walk but here there are some loose holds. The third section contains the thrills. The actual scrambling is either easy or moderate but the route goes along the top of some very exposed slabs. This part is composed of basalt and so is unpleasant in the wet; the holds are sometimes loose.

Luckily there is plenty of room on the summit to relax and

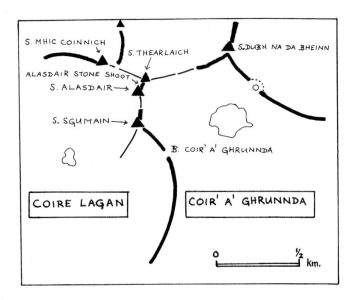

side ridge S.W. from Sgurr Thearlaich

S. Thearlaich	978	3208
The Great Stone Shoot	956	3135
(Coire Lagan) ←		
S. Alasdair	993	3257
dip	921	3023
S. Sgumain	947	3108
B. Coir' a' Ghrunnda	841	2759
(Coire Lagan) ← → (Coir' a' Ghrunnda)		
Sron na Ciche	859	2817

prepare for the descent which seems easier than the way up. At the summit take the opportunity to observe the ridge of Sgurr Thearlaich opposite. Novice scramblers frequently stray down it and can be seen spreadeagled all over the end of the mountain, precariously edging their way off it in various perilous places.

The way off the south end of Mhic Coinnich is also a rock climb (Diff.). A word must be said about Collie's Ledge. This runs from two thirds distance along the ridge of Mhic Coinnich across the face on the Lagan side, to about 6m. (20 ft.) above the Bealach Mhic Coinnich, then exposed scrambling down to it. See also the appendix.

33 Sgurr Alasdair   993m.   (3257 ft.)

Peak of Alexander after Sheriff Alexander Nicolson who made the first ascent of the Great Stone Shoot in 1873.

This king of the Cuillin is shaped as a good summit should be into a final cone, crowned by its topmost cairn. From it is a superbly contrasting panorama. Nearby the curving linked peaks of the main ridge stretching north and south, westwards the wide expanse of sea and island, with the long tangled line of mainland peaks to the east.

Sgurr Alasdair does not lie on the main ridge but on a spur extending from the Alasdair-Thearlaich col to Sgumain and Sron na Ciche. The main ridge runs over Mhic Coinnich, Thearlaich then south-east to the Bealach Coir' an Lochain, cut by the cleft of the Thearlaich-Dubh Gap which is a V. Diff. rock climb.

The south-west ridge of Alasdair is mainly composed of shattered rocks and scree ledges; it appears to be an easy way but low down near Sgurr Sgumain is the "Mauvais Pas", a short pitch of rock climbing (V. Diff.).

With the ridge of Sgurr Thearlaich on the third side, Sgurr Alasdair is thus guarded by rock climbs all round and the only

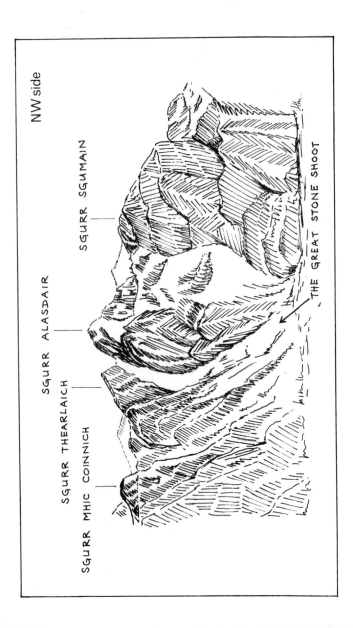

NW side

SGURR MHIC COINNICH

SGURR THEARLAICH

SGURR ALASDAIR

SGURR SGUMAIN

THE GREAT STONE SHOOT

access for the walker and scrambler is to approach via Coire Lagan (Route 31) and to toil up the depths of the Great Stone Shoot. For the inexperienced who merely hope to bag their peak this must be gruelling; for the hillman who is used to scree, it could be a lot worse. Parties in the Shoot at the same time are the main problem. It is possible to ascend without sending stones down but few tread carefully. It cannot be emphasised too strongly that you need to move as delicately as possible when there are others on the scree and to keep a constant vigil for dislodged stones. The easiest way begins on the right hand side and at the narrows it tracks over to the left (upward direction).

A word of warning: the Great Stone Shoot is what its name implies. Its top is out of sight but it obviously funnels out from a narrow neck - scree all the way. In misty conditions care should be taken not to veer out right on to the large area of scree to the south of the shoot which leads to the Alasdair Sgumain col from which rises the south-west ridge with its impassable-to-scramblers mauvais pas.

On reaching the top of the stone shoot, the scree goes over the top and apparently down to Coire a' Ghrunnda. You may look over here but do not attempt to descend it as it ends a little lower at the top of a precipice. On your right, or south-east side, a short easy scramble of about 30m. (100 ft.) leads to the summit. Return the same way.

34 Sgurr Thearlaich   978m.   (3208 ft.)

(Hyaal-uch) Peak of Charles after Charles Pilkington who led the first ascent of this unclimbed and unnamed north top of Alasdair in 1887.

At the top of the Great Stone Shoot there is a steep wall on the left which leads to the ridge of Thearlaich. There are several ways up this wall, all of which are very hard scrambling. If the scree is descended on the Coir' a' Ghrunnda side

Looking north from Sgurr Alasdair.

for about 36m. (120 ft.), near a corner, the way up the wall is a little easier or a traverse can be made to go directly up the nose though this is exposed and, at the time of writing, there are many loose holds. It should be stressed that Sgurr Thearlaich is much harder than Sgurr Alasdair and it is not an option for walkers and those with little experience.

To continue the ridge to Mhic Coinnich is not recommended to scramblers as it is airy, loose and ends with a difficult section down to the col.

35 Sron na Ciche   859m.   (2817 ft.)

Sron na Ciche is the broad shoulder which lies between Coire Lagan and Coir' a' Ghrunnda. It is faced on its north-west side by one of the most magnificent cliffs for climbing that exist in Britain. At the north end it narrows to the Bealach Coir' a' Ghrunnda (see below) which is an easy way between Coire Lagan and Coir' a' Ghrunnda, and from which an ascent of Sgurr Sgumain can be made without difficulty.

To reach the shoulder, follow the Coir' a' Ghrunnda track over the Lagan burn, then make for the end of the shoulder as it comes down at the south-west corner. If you keep to this corner you will find signs of wear and cairns. You continue up this by scree and boulders until abreast a small rock outcrop on the skyline. This is the beginning of the crest above the climbs and is marked by a larger cairn. The way continues, mainly over large boulders, until the summit cairn (not very distinctive) is reached. (2½ hours). Moderate scrambling, easier on the right, leads down to the bealach.

A more attractive way of reaching Bealach Coir' a' Ghrunnda is under the face of Sron na Ciche. Take the track to Coire Lagan but fork right toward the cliff. The track crosses the Lagan burn and, trekking round several climbers' "boulder problems", it goes up scree under the face in a variety of places. Keep round under the climbs and eventually you will find yourself in a gully between the main face and a jumble of blocks in the middle of the scree. From this route you get some good views of the climbs. Look out for the strange lump of rock called the Cioch (Kee-och, ch as in loch, "the breast", from which Sron na Ciche gets its name).

The gully is well marked and easy to follow. Technically the scrambling here is often hard, especially if you are small but it is thoroughly enjoyable, not exposed, and does not last for as long as you might wish.

Above the jammed blocks you continue up the boulders or scree to emerge on the col. It is also a good means of descent. You can keep out nearer to Sgumain on the scree but this is far less interesting and pleasant.

On the other side of the bealach the way to Coir' a' Ghrunnda is down the scree. It is short, marked and cairned; it can also be ascended with moderate effort.

36 Sgurr Sgumain   947m.   (3108 ft.)

(Skoo-men) Stack Peak. This was once the name for all the tops in this area of Coire Lagan - Alasdair, Thearlaich, and Sgumain.

From Bealach Coir' a' Ghrunnda it is easy to reach the summit of Sgurr Sgumain; the way is clear and the scrambling easy. The summit reveals the closeness of Sgurr Alasdair and it will seem tempting to try the south-west ridge but there is a "mauvais pas" of V. Diff. climbing standard on it.

It is possible from the summit to reach the Alasdair - Sgumain col by scrambling down, usually on the Ghrunnda side, then traversing round a few corners and along a basalt sill. One or two moves are moderate to hard but the rest is merely airy, loose and greasy in the wet. Should you decide to do this, then you can make your way down on the Ghrunnda side by going up to the beginning of the rise to Alasdair, then down the scree, either straight down or, keeping under the cliffs,

84

trend towards Bealach Coir' an Lochain.

There is also the alternative of descending on the Lagan side, if visibility is good, but there are rock patches and the scree is wretched: not recommended. By far the best way off Sgumain is to go back to Bealach Coir' a' Ghrunnda and down one of the three routes already described. (Time: To summit, 3 hours).

37 Coir' a' Ghrunnda

The Floored Corrie.

The massive grandeur of this corrie of glaciated slabs and rock faces, with its burn cascading white down the gabbro, is most imposing. Early guide books always urged caution with regard to this corrie but the way is now clearly marked and, if you do not stray, it should be visited for as far as the walker feels comfortable; scramblers can all reach the loch, the bealachs and beyond.

Set out up the moor from the Glen Brittle campsite, as for Coire Lagan, until you reach the first stream; cross this and follow the broad highway. This crosses the large burn coming from Coire Lagan and starts to rise across the end of Sron na Ciche. At a small dip where the rabbits play, there is a neat cairn and the path has more boulders. The track then divides round a shattered rock which looks in mist like a vast cairn. Take the upper track each time it divides, past a cairn on a high rectangular block, always striking up the hillside until you join a traversing track which leads right round and into the west side of the corrie at about 360m. (1200 ft.).

The upward route through scree, boulders and slabs is clear, and is cairned. At one point, when you are close to the stream, the way is scratched up a glacis or angle in the rock. This section is moderate, or perhaps even hard in the wet. More boulders follow, then it levels out to reach the loch at 700m. (2300 ft.). (Time: about 2 hours).

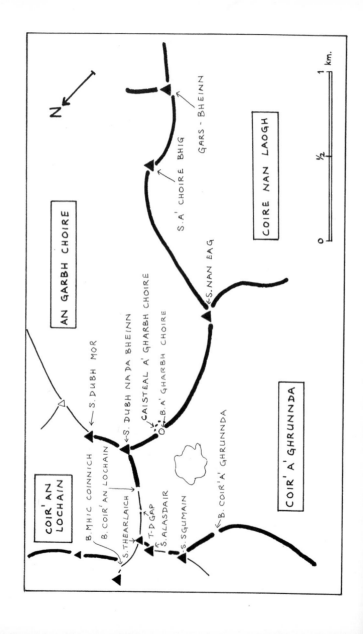

N

AN GARBH CHOIRE

COIR' AN LOCHAIN

COIRE NAN LAOGH

COIR' A' GHRUNNDA

GARS - BHEINN

S.A' CHOIRE BHIG

S. NAN EAG

B.A' GHARBH CHOIRE

CAISTEAL A' GHARBH CHOIRE

S. DUBH NA DA BHEINN

S. DUBH MOR

B. MHIC COINNICH

B. COIR' AN LOCHAIN

S. THEARLAICH

T- D GAP

S. ALASDAIR

S. SGUMAIN

B. COIR' A' GHRUNNDA

0   ½   1 km.

corries	main ridge	metres	feet
	S. Thearlaich	978	3208
	Thearlaich–Dubh gap	c899	2950
	Pinnacle	c908	2980
	B. Coir' an Lochain	855	2806
(Coir' a' Ghrunnda) ← → (Coir' an Lochain)			
	S. Dubh na Da Bheinn	938	3078
		[S. Dubh Mor 944	3096]
	dip	c800	2625
	Caisteal a' Gharbh Choire	829	2719
	B. a' Gharbh Choire	797	2614
(Coir' a' Ghrunnda) ← → (An Garbh Choire)			
	S. nan Eag	924	3031
	dip	773	2537
	S. a' Choire Bhig	875	2872
	dip	c838	2750
	Gars-bheinn	895	2935

In clear weather an unforgettable scene extends before you. On sunny days the colour of the loch seems unbelievable; the bare ice-ground slabs give place to grey scree beneath cliffs which seem deceptively near. Sgumain, Alasdair (though perhaps less impressive from here), the brown, broken slopes of Sgurr Dubh na Da Bheinn, Caisteal a' Gharbh Choire, and finally the mass of Sgurr nan Eag on the right.

From this corrie there is access to four bealachs: Bealach Coir' a' Ghrunnda, the Sgumain - Alasdair col, Bealach Coir' an Lochain, Bealach a' Gharbh Choire. Ascents can be made of Sron na Ciche, Sgumain, Sgurr Dubh na Da Bheinn to the Dubh ridge, Sgurr nan Eag, and continue to follow the last part of the main ridge. You can cross to Coruisk, remembering that you have to get back. The one spot which is denied you is Sgurr Alasdair.

You may wish to cross the Bealach Coir' a' Ghrunnda (Route 35) but otherwise descent is by the way you came. When crossing the jumble of very large blocks, keep to the cairns and scratch marks which more or less traverse through them without too much loss of height. At one point a cairn marks a route downwards. It is possible to follow the sparsely cairned route it marks over the slabs but if it is wet, or you do not like walking on rounded slabs in airy situations, it is best avoided. At the lower end of the jumbled blocks the main track crosses a dyke which supports a natural rock garden with a variety of flowers.

Once out of the corrie and traversing across the moor, watch out for the cairn on the rectangular blocks and shortly afterwards follow the track which is (1978) beginning to appear slanting downwards; otherwise you will go round too far under Sron na Ciche and have to drop down later; it is easy but unnecessary. It takes about $1\frac{1}{2}$ hours down from the loch.

At Loch Coire Lagan. The cliffs of Sron na Ciche with the Cioch
casting its shadow in the centre.

Sgurr Mhic Coinnich.

38 Sgurr Dubh na Da Bheinn   938m. (3070 ft.)

(Doo-na-dah-vain) The Black Peak of the Two Hills.

This peak at the head of Coir' a' Ghrunnda commands fine views of the ridge and especially of the back of Sgurr Alasdair. It is easily ascended from either Bealach Coir' an Lochain or Bealach a' Gharbh Choire.   From the former it is mainly a walk, though route finding in mist can be difficult as the way is not worn.   It is hardly worth trying to keep strictly to the edge.   The picture is different from Bealach a' Gharbh-Choire where there is a fine crest which provides a worthwhile scramble, of all grades of difficulty, up the peridotite. Easier ground is now being worn into a track on the Ghrunnda side if this is preferred.   It is easy to avoid the summit altogether but this would not only miss out a good vantage point but also a sharp and shapely summit in its own right.

39 Sgurr Dubh Mor   944m. (3096 ft.)

The Big Black Peak.

This mountain lies north east of Sgurr Dubh na Da Bheinn and the main ridge.   Together with its smaller neighbour, Sgurr Dubh Beag, it forms the Dubh Ridge which stretches down to Coruisk; it includes moderate rock climbing. It can be reached from Sgurr Dubh na Da Bheinn by easy scrambling across the dip and along the approach which is on the An Garbh-Choire side.   The ascent is scratch-marked but involves one or two hard moves, especially in the wet, and it becomes quite exposed. The summit is an airy viewpoint.

Return by way of Sgurr Dubh na Da Bheinn. The apparently easy gullies down to An Garbh-Choire do not "go".

40 Bealach a' Gharbh Choire   797m. (2614 ft.)

Strictly speaking the pass is between Sgurr nan Eag and Caisteal a' Gharbh Choire (cairn); but as the dips on both sides of the castle are approximately the same height, are

Looking north from Sgurr Dubh na Da Bheinn. Left to right: Sgumain, Alasdair, Thearlaich, Mhic Coinnich.

equally accessible from either corrie, and connect by paths on both sides of the Caisteal, it seems something of a technicality. On the Ghrunnda side there is the beginning of a track, especially to the actual bealach. At the Dubh end there is a tilted block under which you have to squeeze yourself and your loaded rucksack. Perhaps the best choice is to take the Sgurr nan Eag side from Coir' a' Ghrunnda, go round behind the castle and make down the corrie either in the centre or towards the Dubhs.

41 Caisteal a' Gharbh Choire   829m.   (2719 ft.)
The Castle of the Rough Corrie.

This is a prominent knobble of the extremely rough, ginger-brown rock called peridotite. The traverse of its ridge is a rock climb but fun can be had scrambling along many of the ledges on the west side. An easy track passes down and under on the east side and there are many species of mountain flowers to be seen here. The bleached and tattered slings lying beneath, or still attached to, the north end are witness to the fact that it is fairly easy to climb up the south end but that the north end overhangs.

42 Sgurr nan Eag   924m.   (3031 ft.)
The Peak of the Clefts.

Though hardly convenient from base, this mountain can provide an enjoyable scramble without being too serious. There are three main approaches.

The usual ascent and descent is from Coir' a' Ghrunnda. Strike up from the loch to the Bealach a' Gharbh Choire, or directly towards the north-west ridge of the mountain. The crest of the ridge affords a fine position with views sweeping down to Coruisk. The scrambling can be varied from some quite hard moves, though not usually exposed, to some sections of walk up scree paths to the right. There is a surprising

Sgurr Dubh Mor and Sgurr Dubh na Da Bheinn.   Thearlaich-Dubh gap visible on left.

amount of summit ridge before you gain the airy cairn which is not far from the beginning of the descent to the head of Coire nan Laogh.

Another way is the continuation of the ridge from Gars-bheinn. Thirdly, if taken on its own, it can be approached from the track which leads past Coire nan Laogh at about 250m. (800 ft.). Then flog up the tedious scree and boulders of the east side of the mountain which overlooks Coire nan Laogh. You can go further left but the best place is near the rock of the corrie. In reverse this shoulder goes off in a southerly direction only a few minutes from the summit and only about 20m. (70 ft.) lower. One way to recognise the descent is a large bluff of rock on your left hand as you begin to descend. Another is to come upon the top of a deep gash; keep this well to the left. From time to time a cairn marks the place where the descent begins. Unfortunately it often gets carried away and, without this mark, it is all too easy to trot off down to the bealach of Coire nan Laogh. The scrambler is advised not to attempt the complicated descent of the slabs of the corrie for there is much cliff here.

If going down the southerly ridge above Coire nan Laogh you should probably allow 3 hours. The rough descent of the mountain may take about an hour and the trek back to Glen Brittle at least another hour. It is quicker to go back to Coir' a' Ghrunnda and down (2 hours). To go on to Gars-bheinn and down needs $3\frac{1}{2}$ hours, and lots of time and energy in hand.

43 Sgurr a' Choire Bhig   875m.   (2872 ft.)
(Vick) The Peak of the Little Corrie.

This top is on the ridge between Sgurr nan Eag and Gars-bheinn and forms part of the ridge walk between the two. The ridge is narrow enough for a feeling of elevation but not so dramatic as much of the Cuillin. There are no problems in mist concerning route finding except the Bealach Coire nan

Southern end of the ridge. Sgurr Dubh na Da Bheinn on left, over Sgurr nan Eag to Gars-bheinn seen in the centre.

Laogh, which is relatively wide and boulder strewn; it has some cairns and signs of wear.

44 Gars-bheinn   895m.   (2935 ft.)

(Garsh-vain) The Echoing Mountain.

There is an error on some maps which give the height as 910m. but this is to be corrected in the new O.S. editions.

This is the most southerly point of the ridge from where the majority of climbers who embark on the traverse begin their expedition. It commands fine views out to sea and down to Coruisk, so that it is worth continuing a little past the summit to enjoy them to the full.

This mountain is very distant for a Cuillin peak and it feels even further. From Glen Brittle there is the long trek across the moor on the 250m. (800 ft.) path which can be three times as long in wet weather as the deepest splurges of bog are avoided. After crossing the stream coming out of Coire nan Laogh, there is nothing for it but to grind up the south-west shoulder. Long grass and heather give way to scree and boulders. There are no problems; just hard work to the top. There is a tendency to gain the ridge to the west of the summit but the crest is readily identified, though in mist you need to be careful of the crags on the Coruisk side.

From the campsite to the summit you will need 3 to 4 hours. As Coire nan Laogh is not recommended, your best plan is to continue to Sgurr nan Eag (1 hour), along its ridge and descend to Coir' a' Ghrunnda. Otherwise, retreat would be by the eastern edge of the shoulder of Sgurr nan Eag.

45 Coruisk

More properly, Coir' Uisg, pronounced Cor-oosh-k, and very aptly meaning "Water Corrie".

Previously known to shepherds and crofters, the first written reference to Coruisk came early in the nineteenth century and it shortly became known, at least by hearsay, when Sir Walter Scott wrote "The Lord of the Isles" and his poems were illustrated by Turner. This began the tourist trek to Coruisk even before the Cuillin themselves were known. They came by sea, were appalled or impressed, and went away again. A few began to penetrate the fastness of this remote spot and to be touched by the feel of the numinous here.

It is indeed awesome. A deep dark loch nearly 3 km. (2 miles) long and half a kilometre wide. It has been gouged out by glaciers which have worn the slabs, abandoned the perched blocks, and left such dramatic relics of their presence to cause Professor James Forbes to arrive at his pioneering discoveries of glacial action in Britain.

Coruisk lies at the heart of the Cuillin. Two-thirds of the main ridge surrounds it, and the experienced mountaineer can reach it from several points along the whole range. Though the peaks at the head are another 3 km. away (two miles), they dominate the scene. It is surrounded by jagged summits, strewn with boulders, and shows a considerable amount of bare rock. Though not devoid of vegetation as Scott suggested, it is the naked rock which overwhelms the beholder with fear or admiration. It is due to this that heavy rain causes, almost immediately, the walls to stream with water, the torrents of white foam to plunge out of the gloom of the mist above, down to the ebony loch below.

Sheriff Nicolson caught its feeling when he wrote, "What a sight was that seething cauldron and its black environment with the mists rolling down and flying up and winding about and struggling like persecuted ghosts... There leaped out of the grey turmoil the black head of some formidable peak, wildly defiant, and in a moment again it was hidden by the driving mist."

Though the predominant mood is one of darkness, mystery and human insignificance, yet there is another side. When it

98

catches the sun and the loch forms a blue backcloth to the white Arctic Tern chattering above the island; the vegetation, still wet, shines luxuriantly green, and the gabbro glows warm-brown; then it shows another face. One can never do justice to Coruisk; the reader must go for himself. Go, taste and see. But go in small numbers for what is most compelling about Coruisk is its silence.

The ways to arrive at this sanctuary are: by boat; via Glen Sligachan; the walk in from Camusunary over the "Bad Step"; the coast route from Glen Brittle; or by various passes over the ridge. As an introduction the boat trip from Elgol should not be scorned; coming in this way you receive the full impact of this dramatic place. Arriving at sea-level the eye is led up to the rising rock walls, the encircling ridges, to the ser-rated skyline. If arranged with the boatman (at a fee), it may also leave you time to explore. You can walk right round the loch and gain a more complete impression than there is ever time for if arriving any other way. It is usually reckoned to take two hours to walk round the loch.

It may well be thought that so remote a place can only justly be enjoyed if reached by personal effort. There are three approaches for the strong walker.

Perhaps the most rewarding is to take the path up Glen Sli-gachan from the old bridge (signposted "Loch Coruisk"). It is a wild and rough path, giving views of the Black Cuillin Ridge on your right hand; some of the Red Cuillin on your left, and later the sight of Blaven too. It is, however, a very long way, perhaps twice as far as the 11 km. (7 miles) measured on the map, by the time you have avoided all the boulders and inevit-able bog and splash. After about 7 km., past the Lochan Dubha, the path divides and you take the right fork which winds up the ridge Druim Hain to about 305m. (1000 ft.) above sea-level, then down past the lonely Loch a' Choire Riabhaich (ree-ya-vich, Loch of the Brindled Corrie) to the River Scavaig.

This is the route which also gives access to Sgurr na Stri (stree, Hill of Strife). Its south and west faces are steep and dramatic but from the Druim Hain you can walk to the top. Take the traversing path to the left until an obvious cairn on a slabby ridge which overlooks both the loch and the sea. The view is spectacular. From here you can walk or scramble up slabs to the summit. Because of its position, looking right up the loch, and its intermediate height, it is a splendid viewpoint for Blaven and much of the ridge; it is possibly the best one for Loch Coruisk. From the obvious cairn on the traversing track descent to Coruisk is possible but the cairns take you toward the sea over an exposed slab. In clear conditions it would be easier for the walker to slant down on the side of the ridge but it is quite unmarked.

If you do not follow this diversion, care is needed on the top of the Druim Hain that this traversing path is not taken. Continue straight over where there are many cairns though these are not immediately obvious as they lie on slabs. Go on down near the Allt a' Choire Riabhaich and the track will lead to the stepping stones over the River Scavaig. A right fork goes along the north-east side of the loch under the Druim nan Ramh, but you would only choose this way if making a circuit of the loch.

It cannot be too strongly emphasised that, like all routes to Coruisk, it is a very long way; and when you get there it is an even longer trek back. Seven to eight hours would seem reasonable and it may well take longer.

The second route on this side includes the "Bad Step". For this you need to take a car down the A881 Broadford to Elgol road and try to get it on the limited parking space south of Kirkibost where the track says "Camasunary $1\frac{1}{2}$ hours". From here flog uncomfortably across the track of chippings to the isolated beach at Camasunary with its views of Rum and its intense loneliness. There is a bothy here.

Alternatively, you can leave a car at Elgol and take the path so strongly marked (on the map anyway!) along the east side of Loch Scavaig. It seems to offer more than the way in from Kirkibost with views across to Soay, Rum and into Coruisk, and with a chance to watch the seabirds. It is a narrow track, crossing the coast-side high above the sea. It involves virtually no scrambling but in terms of exposure it has its moments. Its main snag is that it is not over rock but mud. It also takes about $1\frac{1}{2}$ hours to reach the bay.

From Camasunary (Cama-soo-nary, The Bay of the Fair Shieling) cross the river by the suspension bridge and continue on a well marked coast track round the south end of Sgurr na Stri. Eschewing one or two temptations left to viewpoints, you rise up with the cairns and look through to Coruisk. The path goes clearly down again, over some rock and arrives at the famous Bad Step. A slab of rock descends straight into Loch Scavaig at this point. Some variations have been made higher up but people who get into difficulties have usually been those who have kept too high and it is best to cross at the classic "step" which is only 5m. (15 ft.) above high water mark. It is clearly scratched, and readily identifiable if you have seen any picture of it.

Take the broad shelf which leads round a corner to above the water. Then a large crack rises up the slab ahead. It is not difficult to scramble up this for the lower lip of the crack forms giant footholds. When the handholds thin out, do not continue up the crack but step left across to a small platform; then down an easy ledge.

It is said to be simpler to find if first tackled from Coruisk, but it is certainly easier to cross when coming from the south. Coming from the north, the first moves off the small platform, with the sea below, may seem airy but stand firmly on the crack with hands on the slab and soon good holds, for hands as well as feet, will be reached.

For either of the ways via Camasunary you should allow 3 hours for the outward journey. All the routes so far described bring you to the east side of the short, but fast and wide, River Scavaig, which takes the waters of Loch Coruisk to the sea. To cross this there is the hazard of the stepping-stones; like all Cuillin rivers, it can rise rapidly and quickly become impassible.

The third walk in, which avoids crossing the ridge, is the so-called "Coast route from Glen Brittle". This is not a leisurely amble by the sea; most walkers agreeing with Alex Small that it is a "gruelling tramp" needing 4 hours for the one way trip. It is rough, up and down, and often wet. While the route is mostly clear, it is significant that the Outdoor Leisure map does not indicate any path, distinct or otherwise. There are one or two spots of easy scrambling and a little mildly airy walking above the sea, otherwise the problems are just the distance.

Take the track to Gars-bheinn. Keep at the height of about 275m. (900 ft.) over the shoulder then go north to just before the Allt a' Chaoich or Mad Burn. Another route is to descend from the track after the Allt Coire nan Laogh and pick up the coast to the east of it. It is then up and down amid the bracken, little ravines and boulders until you also reach the Mad Burn. Ascent or descent is not made beside the burn itself but by the smaller parallel stream to the south west where there is an incipient track. The cliffs of Meall na Cuilce are not for the scrambler; there is little alternative to boulder-hopping along the shore if making for the Memorial Hut. Another possibility is to aim for the point where the Allt a' Chaoich forks at about 168m. (550 ft.). Curve round on the north-west of Meall na Cuilce to reach the loch-side. All this area is a trackless wilderness and difficult to cross in mist.

Finally there are the ways to Coruisk that go across the ridge. These may include peaks and involve rock climbing.

A lot depends on your strength, ability, experience, and how much you are carrying. None is clearly marked all the way; all demand an ability to cope with the rough terrain and stamina to take you there and back. The round trip is a long day for anyone and will need at least 12 hours.

Probably the most popular is over Bealach Coire na Banachdich (Route 28), down the long scree on the other side, then following the side of the burn where there is some semblance of a track. After this comes a long tramp beside the main river, followed by the loch itself, which is fairly well marked but very wet. The word "ford" on the map bears no relation to the frequency with which you have to ford your way along the path. Allow 5 hours to the hut; it could take longer in poor conditions.

The return can be by the coast route or by An Garbh Choire (An-garve-corrie, The Rough Corrie) if you can face another 800m. (2600 ft.) of ascent. The latter can also be used as a way over. To reach the bealach, see Routes 37 and 40.

In one sense the route up or down this corrie is quite straightforward as you can keep near the bottom of the V. However, in the upper reaches it is a mass of tumbled boulders, some seeming as large as a house, and scrambling over these is a time-consuming and sometimes precarious business. The rock is mainly peridotite and the devastation this causes the hands can last for days. Nevertheless, it is a fine corrie with views of the end of the ridge. Now and then you come upon a little rock garden bright with flowers in spring and summer. There is always the feeling that some rarity may turn up here and, together with the approach from Coir' a' Ghrunnda, it is amongst the most worthwhile places for those with an interest in mountain flowers.

If using this way to return from Loch Coruisk watch out for the slabs of the Dubh ridge; keeping these on your right, set off up the burn which comes down from the main corrie at about 150m. (500 ft.). Cairns appear at about 330m. to 600m. (1100 ft. to 2000 ft.) but they are not continuous. Near the top the way is said to be easier on the flank of Sgurr Dubh but in ascent it is preferable to scramble over the blocks. Make for either side of Caisteal a' Gharbh Choire and go down Coir' a' Ghrunnda. See Route 37.

Bealach na Glaic Mhor is another possibility as a way over the ridge but, like Bealach Coire na Banachdich, its scree does not make it ideal for a two-way trip and if used one way there are transport problems. In mist the route over the bealach can be tricky.

To sum up, a preliminary visit by boat might be useful. Then, at a later date, a strong party might go by way of Bealach Coire na Banachdich and return either by the coast route or An Garbh Choire. Whatever the route, all who go to Coruisk will look back on the visit as one of the memorable events amongst many memorable occasions in the Cuillin.

APPENDIX

The following routes are sometimes undertaken by parties with some rock climbing experience. A few notes are included to give some indication of what is involved.

Sgurr nan Gillean - West Ridge

The only difficulty here is the short section of shattered ridge which contains the "Gendarme". There are various ways of passing it; the usual way is to traverse it on the Coir' a' Bhasteir side but some find it less exposed just along the line of its base on the Lota Corrie side.

Bidein Druim nan Ramh

The traverse of this peak is best left to the climbers but it is easy to scramble to the top of the West Peak and down slabs to the dip. You can descend the gully between the West and the Central tops.

When approached from the north the North Peak is a scramble from the ridge. It is easy on the Harta Corrie side for about 60m. (200 ft.), but there is a rather exposed wall near the top. Return by the same route.

Sgurr a' Mhadaidh - Foxes Rake

Nearly 300m. (1000 ft.) of scrambling, originally "Mod.", now downgraded to "Easy". It makes a way up the face where the angle is low and the sense of exposure not great; there are few places of technical interest and it is dangerously loose, often slabby, and usually wet. The holds tend to be not very positive and there is a total absence of belays should they be required. The route is difficult to find even on a clear day.

Sgurr Mhic Coinnich - Collie's Ledge

A dyke traverse leading from Bealach Mhic Coinnich to part way along the ridge, omitting the summit. It starts 6m. (20 ft.) above the col and leads round to the left along the west face. It has two thin bits but otherwise depends on how well members of the party like this sort of exposed traverse; a leader cannot offer much assistance.

Sgurr Alasdair - South-West Ridge

The only difficulty on this loose and shattered ridge is the "mauvais pas" which is V. Diff. It can be avoided by traversing further along the Coir' a' Ghrunnda side and up a chimney. After this a leftward rising slant should be made to the crest which is very exposed and slippery when wet.

CONTOUR EQUIVALENTS

1 metre = 3.28 ft. approx.
1 foot = 0.30 metre approx.

feet	metres	feet	metres
5	1.5	1300	396
10	3	1400	427
20	6	1500	457
30	9	1600	488
40	12	1700	518
50	15	1800	549
60	18	1900	579
70	21	2000	610
80	24	2100	640
90	27	2200	671
100	30	2300	701
200	61	2400	732
300	91	2500	762
400	122	2600	792
500	152	2700	823
600	183	2800	853
700	213	2900	884
800	244	3000	914
900	274	3100	945
1000	305	3200	975
1100	335	3300	1006
1200	366		

MOUNTAIN CODE

Issued by the Mountaineering Council for Scotland.

BEFORE YOU GO
Learn the use of map and compass
Know the weather signs and local forecast
Plan within your capabilities
Know simple first aid and the symptoms of exposure
Know the mountain distress signals
Know the Country Code

WHEN YOU GO
Never go alone
Leave written word of your route and report your return
Take windproofs, woollens, and survival bag
Take map and compass, torch and food
Wear climbing boots
Keep alert all day

IF THERE IS SNOW ON THE HILLS
Always have an ice-axe for each person
Carry a climbing rope and know the correct use of rope and ice-axe
Learn to recognise dangerous snow slopes

Not infrequently climbers and walkers cause the rescue services to be called out unnecessarily because no one knew that they did not intend to return that night or because plans were changed. Always leave a message in case of the former, and of the possibility of the latter. If you think you may have caused concern, telephone the police in case there is a search on for you.

MOUNTAIN RESCUE

The mountain rescue post is at GLEN BRITTLE HOUSE
It is not at the campsite which does not have a telephone.

A stretcher and first aid are kept at the Coruisk Memorial Hut
but this is locked except when the hut is in use.

There are public telephone boxes at Glen Brittle House,
Sligachan Hotel, Elgol and Torrin. If help is required, telephone the police at Portree 2888. Dialling 999 connects the
caller to Inverness police.

MOUNTAIN DISTRESS SIGNALS
Six blasts of a whistle, flashes of a torch, or even shouts, in
a minute. Then silence for a minute. Then repeat.
Red flare.

SUMMARY OF ROUTES DESCRIBED